BEFORE
Love
DIES

Getting Your Needs Met in Relationships

LARRY J. RUSSELL, M.A.

LEGACY
PUBLISHERS INTERNATIONAL

BEFORE *Love* DIES

Getting Your Needs Met in Relationships

BEFORE LOVE DIES
ISBN 1-880809-93-1
Printed in the United States of America
Copyright © 2004 by Larry Russell

Legacy Publishers International
1301 South Clinton Street
Denver, CO 80247
Phone: 303-283-7480 FAX: 303-283-7536

Library of Congress Cataloging-in-Publication Data Pending

Cover Design: Tony Laidig, www.thirstydirt.com

1 2 3 4 5 6 7 8 9 10 11 / 09 08 07 06 05 04

Dedication

I dedicate this book:

To my wife Lorrie, for helping me heal from the pain of a failed relationship and for providing me with a loving environment in which to flourish and grow as a husband, father, and pastor. She has truly been the wind beneath my wings, as she supported the development and content of this book, much of which has been tested in the laboratory of our lives together. Thank you, Sweetheart, for the development of this dream together.

To Jared and Carrie, our children, for allowing us the space and time to figure out how to successfully function as a stepfamily and to grow together in a loving, vibrant relationship, and for providing hope to other children of fractured families who out of the ashes can become healthy adults who will settle for no less than the relationship described in this book.

Acknowledgments

I gratefully acknowledge:

Susie Zupancic and Cara Hendricks, who transcribed many hours of teaching tapes that formed the basis for this book.

Dennis and Michele Leonard, publishers of Legacy Publishers International, who encouraged me to put my years of experience in counseling and teaching on marriage onto paper. Without their love and support, this project might never have been completed.

The countless audiences, in seminars, classes, and conferences, who allowed me to test this material in their lives.

The many counseling clients who helped me sharpen the edge of the techniques presented in this book by successfully implementing them in the laboratory of their lives.

The seven godly men who surround me as accountability partners and hold me responsible for living out the biblical principles contained in this book.

Most importantly, my heavenly Father, who so many times lovingly restored me when I failed and fell short of His purpose for my life.

Contents

Foreword

By Lorrie Russell

*I*t breaks my heart to watch the countless numbers of divorced men and women who remarry, just to repeat the same mistakes over again and bring additional devastation to their children, extended families, and friends. Divorce is devastating.

I viewed firsthand the tears in my husband's eyes and the pain in his heart every time we drove away after dropping his children off at their mother's house after weekend visitation, the holidays we missed out on, and the special moments our children will never forget. As the weeks turned into months, and the months turned into years, it seemed that the pain would never cease. But over time God turned the pain into joy, as we were able to take our own failures and use them to help others heal.

God, in His infinite wisdom, knows the pain that divorce causes, and that's why He does not recommend it. However, it must sadden Him even more when a couple who has been married for years and appears outwardly content, has hidden deep inside them a hatred or disdain for their spouse, unforgiveness, discontentment, and other such destructive sentiments. This is not how a godly marriage was meant to function.

Larry and I learned that we could not build a strong marriage with tools that were broken, bruised, or battered. A house that will be strong and solid must be built with good tools. It will need the strongest of foundations, the most durable of walls, and it must be topped off with a most beautiful ceiling where God can be glorified. It blesses me to have a husband who has devoted his life to giving couples biblical tools with which to build a marriage that will withstand the most violent storms that come their way, and I have been honored to be part of that ministry. Together, it has been our privilege to speak all over the world on marriage and stepfamily issues.

I love to watch the response of the audiences when Larry gets to the part of his presentation where he says, "If I would have known in my first marriage what I know now, I could have saved that marriage. It died from a lack of knowledge." Later, many ask me how I feel about that statement. The truth is that I'm thankful Larry feels that way, because I know that he will do everything possible to make our marriage all that God designed it to be.

Larry and I both believe that if two people want to make their relationship work, and they are willing to put forth the necessary effort, it can be done. We are living proof that this is true because we have been married now for twenty-two years, and we are looking forward to many more good years together.

A good marriage doesn't just happen, and yet most of us have spent more time preparing for our individual careers than we have for the two most important roles God has assigned to us, that of spouse and parent. Why is that? It should be important to each of us that we be a private success, as well as a public success. I consider myself to be a blessed woman, wife of a man who loves God and loves me and walks out in daily life what he teaches others. He is my best friend, and I look forward to sharing my life with him until the Almighty takes one of us home.

Introduction

$\mathcal{I}$t is always important for a reader to know how an author learned what he or she is attempting to teach others through a book. My knowledge of matters related to a successful marriage came from several areas. First, I have a Master's Degree in Guidance and Counseling, Marriage and Family Track from the University of Colorado. In addition to my education, I have done approximately fourteen thousand hours of paid therapy, as well as countless hours of volunteer counseling in a variety of settings, and there isn't much I haven't encountered in those sessions. Also, my wife Lorrie and I have taught marriage seminars here in this country and in many other places around the world for many years. In recent years, we are working more with marriage problems within the clergy. These particular teachings come out of an experience we called the Marriage University in which we taught couples on issues relating to marriage in a seminar setting.

However, my real expertise comes from the laboratory of life. In that regard, I am both a failure and a success. In my first attempt at marriage, I failed, and that thirteen-year relationship ended in divorce. I later came to appreciate how this fact hurt God's heart, and I repented for having sinned in this way against His will.

God was more than ready to forgive me when I became willing to recognize my wrongdoing in this regard. He has said:

My dear children, I write this to you so that you will not sin. But if anybody does sin, we have one who speaks to the Father in our defense—Jesus Christ, the Righteous One. He is the atoning sacrifice for our sins, and not only for ours but for the sins of the whole world. 1 John 2:1-2

If we walk in the light, as he is in the light, we have fellowship with one another, and the blood of Jesus, his Son, purifies us from all sin. 1 John 1:7

God has forgiven me for ending my first marriage in divorce, but if I had known then what I know now, I am confident that I could have made that first marriage work. But I didn't know, for that was long before I became a pastor or counselor.

The fact that I failed God in this way and that He was so gracious to forgive me gave me a desire to dedicate much of my life to help others avoid the mistakes I made. This led to my ministry of marriage counseling, to the marriage seminars, to the work with ministry marriages in trouble, and now to this book.

My second marriage has become a success story. Lorrie and I have been married now for more than twenty years, and it has been an incredible experience for us both. She, too, holds a Master's Degree in Marriage and Family Therapy from the University of Colorado, and together we have put to the test in our own daily lives everything that we teach others. We are living proof that these teachings work.

Lorrie is my best friend in all the world as well as my lover. She believed I could be what I now am until I became it. She has been the wind beneath my wings, supplying just enough air to lift me without ever pushing me too much. It is a privilege to have this godly lady by my side as together we move into our second twenty years of life together. As you can imagine, her contribution to this book is immeasurable.

There are two important things that I want to state to the reader at the outset of this book: (1) Lorrie and I never take divorce lightly, and we never advocate it. We have seen the pain divorce has caused others, and we ourselves have had to live with the pain of divorce. Make every effort to work out your differences rather than simply choosing to end your marriage, and (2) My goal in this book is to point you back to our Father and to allow His Word, the Bible, to be your teacher. In this book, I will present some techniques that you might want to employ, and I will tell you about our failures and our successes. My most important goal, however, is to point you to God and allow Him to become the teacher in your marriage. If He is your teacher, your marriage can become all that He has designed it to be.

Larry J. Russell

The Foundations of Marriage

(Or How to Get It Right)

Therefore everyone who hears these words of mine and puts them into prac-
tice is like a wise man who built his house on the rock. The rain came down,
the streams rose, and the winds blew and beat against that house; yet it did
not fall, because it had its foundation on the rock. But everyone who hears
these words of mine and does not put them into practice is like a foolish man
who built his house on sand. The rain came, the streams rose, and the winds
blew and beat against that house, and it fell with a great crash.
Matthew 7:24-27

Jesus spoke of two new houses that looked very much alike. If the storms He also spoke of had not come, these two houses might have seemed to most observers to be equal in quality. But storms do come in life, and when they came in this case, one of the two houses was not able to withstand the accompanying winds and rain. That house fell, and it fell *"with a great crash."*

In so many ways, the houses had seemed alike, but the great difference had been that one was built on sand, and the other was built on rock. A good foundation makes all the difference. Get the foundation right, and you can build a beautiful house that lasts. Fail to get the foundation right, and the most beautiful of houses will not last very long.

In the very same way, marriage, if it is to be successful, requires a firm foundation upon which it can stand. It must be built on the right stuff.

If we can give attention to the proper elements of a solid foundation, we can avoid many of the headaches and heartaches that inevitably come with any neglected relationship.

Just what is the proper foundation for a marriage? How can we build a quality marriage, one that will stand the test of time? Fortunately for us, God has left us many good teachings in His Word on this all-important subject. Since He instituted marriage, we need to know what *He* had in mind in the first place.

Something has to change. Modern Americans are spending great sums of money on their weddings these days, but because those weddings are not built upon the proper foundation, many then have to spend great sums of money on their divorces—sometimes only months or years later. If we would be willing to spend the time and effort necessary to work on what comes between the marriage and the divorce—the daily life of the marriage—we could make the marriage the success it can and should be. If we can give attention to the proper elements of a solid foundation, we can avoid many of the headaches and heartaches that inevitably come with any neglected relationship.

There are, to my way of thinking, five important elements necessary to establishing a proper foundation for marriage before we can even think of building a beautiful life together. In this chapter, let us concentrate on these foundational aspects of marriage, and then, in subsequent chapters, we can go on to other things of mutual interest. Some might think that sexuality, money matters, communication or power issues are more important. Indeed, they are often cited as the *most* important elements in any marriage. But, as with everything else, unless we can grasp the essentials, it is impossible to move on to other concerns.

1. Your Marriage Must Be a Covenant Marriage

The first essential element in the foundation of a successful marriage is covenant. A covenant is a promise, an agreement, a contract, or a pledge. In the case of marriage, a covenant is a pledge made to one another before God, and God considers that pledge to be an unbreakable one. That's where most modern men and women differ from God, and this is also where the first crack often appears in the marriage foundation.

When two individuals stand before an altar making their public promises of fidelity to each other, they are too often thinking that if the marriage doesn't work out they can always get a divorce. In their mind, there is always a way out. The problem with having such an easy exit is that when the going gets rough one or the other of the marriage partners will take it.

My experience is that anyone I counseled with before marriage who said, "If this doesn't work out, we can always get a divorce," generally did. Marriage has its ups and downs and its difficult moments, and if we can simply divorce every time things are not going well, no marriage will last.

Providing for a way out is not covenant. Covenant is not a garment that we can put on and take off at will. It's not something that we just try on for size or wear for a while to see if we like it or not. A marriage covenant is a life-long commitment, and we cannot choose to cast it off simply because it has grown a little moth-eaten and frayed at the edges.

When we commit to someone in marriage, that commitment still stands when their hair begins to turn gray and when their figure begins to appear a little frumpy. When you say "I DO," that means, "When you take your last breath, I'll be there by your side." That's real covenant, and that's what God is looking for in your marriage.

It took me a while to come to the realization of this truth, and Lorrie got there months ahead of me. We were taking a class a local pastor was conducting, and his very first teaching was on covenant.

"Are you in covenant with me?" I asked Lorrie after that session.

"No way!" she said.

"Are you in covenant with *me*?" she turned the question back on me.

"No way!" I had to admit. In my mind I had a whole list of things, and if she did any of them, I was out of there. I also had a whole list of things she'd better do, and, again, if she didn't do them, I was out of there.

What did this pastor mean by covenant? It sounded so impractical, and if I was anything it was practical. I would have to count the costs before making any such serious decision.

What if Lorrie converted to Buddhism and I couldn't agree with her new beliefs? What if she developed a brain tumor and became an invalid and I had to push her around in a wheelchair the rest of her life? If, at some point, she didn't even know who I was anymore, could I still stick by her? Or would I leave her with a caregiver and look for another wife?

What if Lorrie had an affair? Could I forgive her? What if she became a drug addict or an alcoholic? Could I bear that?

This was a difficult decision for me, but eventually I became convinced that God wanted me to make a full commitment to my wife—no matter what came in the future. At the end of five months of wrestling with this issue, I was ready for a marriage covenant.

"I'm in," I said. "You've got me. I'll be here when you take your last breath. You can count on it.

"I don't care how you might look in the future or what you will be like otherwise at that point. When you take your last breath, I'll be there. You can take it to the bank."

This was a critical point in the development of our relationship. We had turned a corner and would never look back. Oh, that many others could make that same commitment!

Sadly, we Americans are all part of a throwaway society. If we don't like something, or if it seems to have served its purpose, we just shed ourselves of it and go on. The same is true of marriage. It seems easy for men and women to break their marriage vows today—when it seems convenient for them to do so. It's time that we learn what it means to go the distance, to be faithful "till death do us part."

To Lorrie and me, having a covenant marriage meant that we were connected, and we were connected in a way that we could not be separated again. When we came to the end of our journey here on earth, we would still be together. There was no doubt about it.

Many of us build what I have come to call security fences around our relationship. The problem is that the fence is full of gates that might open a way of escape. I don't object to gates that are clearly labeled and are supported by scripture. It's the gates that are hidden and known only to one partner that can spell disaster to a relationship. Lorrie and I chose not to have any gates at all in our fence and to spend the rest of our lives together in covenant, regardless of the circumstances life might present to us.

In Old Testament times, there was something called a salt covenant. When a man wanted to make a covenant with another, he would reach into a pouch at his waist containing salt, take out some salt and put it into the pouch of the other person. That person took salt from his pouch and transferred it to the pouch of the first man with the understanding that the covenant could not be broken unless each could identify and remove the original grains of salt from the pouch of the other. We all know that would be impossible. Therefore the covenant was endless.

This tradition led to salt being used in covenant-making in weddings as well. The groom brought a vial of salt from his home, and the bride brought a vial of salt from her home, and those vials were poured together into a vase that could then be placed prominently in the marital home. The message of the vase was that when difficult times came (and they always come) the commingled grains of salt were a reminder that the two of them were committed to each other to the end.

Each of us should freeze-frame the words spoken at our marriage ceremony and then replay them when tough times come our way. It's easy to be committed when everything is going smoothly, but true covenant relationship stands even when all hell breaks loose around us. Eliminate all of the escape hatches, and make a full commitment to your marriage—until death parts you.

2. Your Marriage Must Be Based on Trust

The second element of the proper foundation for a successful marriage is trust. Trust must be earned, and it can also be fractured.

One of the areas that most hurts mutual trust is the way we treat money. Do you hide money from each other? Men, especially, are guilty of this. They buy something they know their wife would not like them to spend money on, and then they hide it from her. Women sneak a new dress into the closet, hoping that their husband will not notice.

I also have a master's degree in business education, and for some years I operated my own tax-preparation service. One couple brought me what was supposed to be all of their financial records, but then the wife showed up the next day with a lot more records. These were her private expenditures, and the husband knew nothing about them. That type of secrecy and breaking of trust is deadly to any marriage. Anytime a spouse misuses money, steals money, or spends money that was intended for the family good on something else, trust is fractured.

Another example of broken trust is with extramarital affairs. The statistics on just how many extramarital affairs occur in this country are astounding. Some people don't go that far, but they do have an affair of the mind, an affair of the emotions, by getting too close to somebody at work.

These days such an affair often begins to take form through emails and escalates from there. When this happens, many people mistakenly believe that they have found their "true soul mate." It seems only natural for them to take the relationship further and to connect with this new person in other ways.

Thus, affairs of the mind very often lead to affairs of the flesh, and people who have just flirted with danger suddenly become sexually involved. Whether the marriage survives this affair or not, an important trust has been broken.

We would like to think that such things do not happen in the Church, but, unfortunately, it's not true. Not only is it happening in the Church; it is happening within the clergy. Clearly God is not pleased with this turn of events.

Another area in which trust can be easily fractured in the marriage is through lying to each other. Lies seem to come so easily to our fallen nature that in much of the world lying is expected and accepted as normal behavior. To Christians, lying is unacceptable.

There is only one place in the Bible where sin is ranked in any way. It is found in Proverbs 6, and it says:

There are six things the Lord hates. Proverbs 6:16 NIV

Amazingly, two of these *"things the Lord hates"* involve lying: *"a lying tongue"* (verse 17) and *"a false witness who pours out lies"* (verse 19). Lying is clearly unacceptable to God, and for good reason. It is a very destructive behavior and one that can have devastating effects upon a marriage.

A final area in which trust can be fractured in the marriage is with broken promises. In my counseling sessions with troubled couples I have often heard phrases like, "You said you would _____ , and you didn't."

Men are particularly guilty of this. We talk out loud about all of the things we're "going to do," and, at the end of the day, our wives want to know why we haven't done them. We need to learn not to promise what we either cannot deliver or don't intend to deliver.

Broken promises in the marriage might involve something as simple as mowing the lawn or repairing something in the house, or it could be as serious as a promise to more fully meet each other's emotional needs. It could be spending more time with the children. It could be taking an interest and lending a helping hand in each other's chosen pursuits. Whatever the particular issue involved, when trust is broken, the result can be dramatic.

We need to learn not to promise what we either cannot deliver or don't intend to deliver.

Suddenly, two people who have become lovers and partners for life have become each other's enemies. Now, when you are seated at the table to eat, instead of seeing across from you the person of your dreams, you are looking into the face of an adversary.

In perfect love, there is no fear (see 1 John 4:18), but when bonds of trust are broken, fear enters the relationship, and we actually begin to fear our mates and what we will become with them by our side. When this happens, something must be done to restore trust, or the marriage is doomed.

The Price of Restoring Trust

The price of restoring trust varies with every situation, and the wronged partner must be given the privilege of naming it. The questions I like to ask are: "What is your price for restored trust?" and "When will it be paid?" The answers to those two questions are crucial.

If I were to have an affair, for example, it would become difficult for Lorrie to trust me as she had before. I might ask her what it would take to restore the trust we had enjoyed, and I might not like her answer. But I would need to give it careful consideration and eventually act on it in some acceptable way if I hoped to keep her as my wife.

She might say, for example, that she needed the liberty to follow me and see where I was going, the liberty to go through my billfold to see what was there, to examine the mail I received, to look through my briefcase, and to ask me any question she felt the need to ask—all without me becoming upset or defensive. She might need the right to pry into my life at any and every level without me resenting it.

If I were going to be late getting home, she might need to know a telephone number (a landline) where I could be reached so that she could call and see if I was really there. If she felt the need to do that, I would have to respond. Whatever it took to restore trust is what I would need to do.

If I had been irresponsible with money, I might not be able to manage my checkbook for a while. Or I might have to give up the privilege of carrying my debit or credit card until I had learned to use it more responsibly.

If a husband takes the family savings and goes and gambles it away, and then he wants with all of his heart to restore the trust his wife and children had in him, he may have to give up control of the family finances for a time. That may be the price he has to pay.

There is a flip side to this. None of us wants to have to pay for some failure for the rest of our lives. Therefore, when we establish with a mate what price will be expected in order to restore trust, we must also establish a time limit. When will that price be satisfied?

It would not be fair for a spouse to respond, "When I feel like it." Trust is not a feeling but rather a deliberate act of our will, a decision that we make based on prevailing circumstances. Unless we can know up front that the price we pay has a time limit, it may seem hopeless and not worth the effort. The price of restored trust must be reasonable.

"I need you to do this for six months," a spouse might say, or "I think one year would be an acceptable time limit." Both need to agree that the demand is reasonable, or it will only lead to more friction in the marriage. And none of us needs that.

An important note to all of this is that the price for restoring trust must never become a means of control used against the offending party, or additional harm will be done to the relationship (more on this later).

The Bible has much to say about trust, and since my journey toward excellence in marriage, both personally and professionally, has been to discover what God says about it and put it into practice, the Bible teaching on this subject has made a great impact upon my life.

One thing the Bible says about trust turned my theology upside down:

Love...always trusts. 1 Corinthians 13:6-7

Once a year I spend some time alone with God on a beach in California, and part of what I do during that time is to look for ways to improve our marriage. On one of those occasions, I was nearing my time to return home when I sensed that God had something important He wanted to say to me.

As I was examining my heart, I had found that there were some pockets of pain still there from the past that had not been dealt with, and I wasn't sure what to do with them. I had forgiven Lorrie for the little things that had offended me. I was sure of that. Why, then, was I feeling this pain?

In time, I realized that I had purposely left some pain there as a protection from further hurt. If I opened myself up totally to Lorrie, I might be hurt again. What I needed to do now was to make myself totally vulnerable to her again.

This is true with any great relationship. If we are to walk close to each other, with our hearts and lives intertwined, we must remove the pockets of pain that periodically trouble us so that we can go on to deeper intimacies.

"What do I need to do, God?" I prayed. It was then that He began to speak to me from First Corinthians 13.

If we are to walk close to each other, with our hearts and lives intertwined, we must remove the pockets of pain that periodically trouble us so that we can go on to deeper intimacies.

I had read that passage over and over. Each year I pick out a particular passage from the Bible that I consider to be crucial to our marriage success, and I work all year on being able to put that teaching into practice. This was the passage I had committed myself to work on for that particular year, and I had told Lorrie in her Valentine's Day card what I intended to do. More than that, this was a commitment to God. I wanted more of His love in my heart, for Lorrie, and also for everyone else.

Now, as I read the passage once again, something new jumped out at me: *"Love always trusts."* If "love always trusts," then I needed to get rid of my hurts—and quickly.

I jumped in the car and drove to the seashore, where I could walk out onto a pier. There, figuratively, I took that hurt I had discovered hidden in my heart, threw it over the railing, and watched as the waves carried it far away from me. It worked. I never felt that pain again.

Another biblical passage that I love on this subject is found in Colossians 3. There Paul spoke of the need to clothe ourselves with such things as humility and patience, to forgive, and to *"put on love"*:

> *Therefore, as God's chosen people, holy and dearly loved, clothe yourselves with compassion, kindness, humility, gentleness and patience. Bear with each other and forgive whatever grievances you may have against one another. Forgive as the Lord forgave you. And over all these virtues put on love, which binds them all together in perfect unity.* Colossians 3:12-14

I could not think of any more delightful way to express it. We need to just clothe ourselves with it, and then to wrap it all together with love.

The Bible is *"a lamp to my feet"* and *"a light for my path"* (Psalm 119:105). It is my guidebook for living, my road map through life. Because it tells me that *"love always trusts,"* that settles it. I have to trust.

3. Your Marriage Must Be Based on the Ability to Forgive

The third element that makes up a firm foundation for a successful marriage is the ability to forgive, and this is a tough one for many. They believe that if they forgive their spouse, the other person has won. But this is not true at all. When you forgive, you are not giving in to the desires of the other person, and you are not forgiving for their sake. You are doing it for your own peace of mind.

Every time you forgive, you win. You free yourself of the poisons of bitterness and hatred, poisons that can very literally destroy your very body and soul. Forgiveness means finding freedom from the past in God's way.

When couples come to me for counseling, I can always be sure that this subject of forgiveness will have to be dealt with at some point. It may have to be done during the very first session, or it can sometimes wait until a subsequent session, but it must always be done. At some point, each marriage partner must deal with the fact that a spouse has disappointed them in the past, and forgiveness is in order if any resolution is hoped for.

Today and tomorrow have their own challenges, and they must not be held hostage to our yesterdays.

In many marriages, unfortunately, the past is being allowed to disrupt the present and to prevent the future. It's a little like trying to drive a car while always looking out the rear window. If you do it, sooner or later you will have an accident or cause an accident—or both.

Today and tomorrow have their own challenges, and they must not be held hostage to our yesterdays. It is only after you have pulled the curtain on the past that you can concentrate on the here and now and chart a suitable course for the future.

When the issues of the day come up, someone always seems to pull out the big guns of the past and starts firing. It is time to let the past be the past and to get on with the business of living. After all, life is too short to continually live in bitterness and unforgiveness.

What Is Forgiveness?

My homespun definition of forgiveness is simple: Remembering the past without pain. If the past brings up painful memories, it isn't over yet. God has said:

As far as the east is from the west, so far has he removed our transgressions from us. Psalm 103:12

When you travel north, you eventually reach the North Pole, and then you are suddenly heading south. In the same way, when you travel south, you eventually reach the South Pole, and then you're traveling North. But you can travel east forever and never be heading west, and you can travel west forever and never be heading east. Still, God says that He puts our sins away from us as far as the east is from the west, and also that He puts them into the sea of forgetfulness and remembers them against us no more:

You will again have compassion on us; you will tread out sins underfoot and hurl all our iniquities into the depths of the sea. Micah 7:19

Mortals that we are, it is obviously very difficult to totally erase something from our memories. We do remember the past. But if and when we can remember it without pain we have succeeded in forgiving.

When people come to me for counseling, I sometimes ask them, "Is that former relationship (with a spouse or lover) over with?"

They invariable answer, "Yes."

"Is it really?" I prod.

"Yes," they insist.

"It is? Totally over with?" I ask again.

"Yes, it's all over," they say.

As I probe in this way, I am looking into their eyes for signs that what they perhaps thought was over is not really over at all. My probing sometimes touches sore spots, and then I see the sudden flashes of pain, the reddening and moistening of the eyes, and the change in the voice, and I know I have hit upon a hidden truth.

"It's not over yet, is it?" I ask again.

"No," they admit. "It's not over."

If the pain is still there, and I can reach in and tap it, then it's not over. If on the other hand, we remember the past only in the chronological sense, then it's okay. It happened, but it's over, and we're moving on with life. That is a healthy attitude toward the past.

Why I Am Qualified to Teach Forgiveness

I grew up a very angry and resentful young man, knowing little or nothing about forgiveness. So why am I qualified to write on this important subject? I, who could not forgive, received the ability to forgive, and you can too.

My earliest memory is of a time when I was only three years old, and we were living in a small coastal town in California. I was very angry with my mom that day. In fact, I was furious.

Perched on the toilet in the bathroom with the bathroom door closed in front of me, such a strong urge came over me to speak some sort of profanity that I groped for words. Since no one in our family ever used profanity, I could think of no profane words to say. Still, I was bursting with anger and wanting to express it somehow.

"Oh, poop!" I said. It was the best attempt I could make at that young age at cursing, and cursing is what I so desperately wanted to do. This scene seemed to set the stage for my life.

From the age of three until the age of thirty-three, the years of my life were marked by negative events. These were the milestones I remembered along life's way. To my way of thinking, my life had been marred by abuse of many kinds, and these thoughts were stored up inside me like toxic chemicals. The pain of it all became unbearable at times, and yet it could not find an outlet.

This all reached a climax one day when I came to the realization that my mother had never really loved me. She should have, and she could have, but she didn't. Why didn't she? And could I ever forgive her for that?

Even after I became a believer in Christ, I still hated my mother. This feeling was so intense that I wondered if it might not keep me out of heaven. If so, what could I do about it? I didn't know.

It wasn't that I didn't *want* to forgive. I was an adult now, and I knew that I should forgive, but I just didn't know how to go about it. How could I get out all of that anger and pain? This frustration continued for many years.

When Lorrie and I were doing our graduate studies together at the University of Colorado, we took a rather strange class. The lights were dimmed, and we were instructed to imagine ourselves locked in a cell within a castle on a moor with big ferns all around it. We were first to saw our way out of that cell, and we did this. Next, we were to make our way out of the castle, and we did this. Then, we were to look for bitter roots of unforgiveness that were left at the base of some huge vines. We were to think of things we had been unable to forgive and then to find and pull up the corresponding bitter root and then release it.

I thought I actually might be onto something, and I pulled and pulled and released and released. But the next morning my unforgiveness and feelings of anger for my mother and others were still with me.

It wasn't that I hadn't tried many times already. I cannot count the number of times I went to the altar because of this matter. There I would do everything I knew to do, but to no avail.

"Leave it on the altar," I was told, so I did. Then, as I turned to walk away, it seemed that the unforgiveness had strings attached to the heels of my shoes. It followed me back to my seat and refused to let me go. As you can imagine, this left me in total despair.

Eventually I was assigned to teach a Sunday school class, and one Sunday the lesson was on forgiveness. As I stood before the class that day, trying to present the lesson as best I could, I began to weep from the pain of my own unforgiveness. In despair, I sat down in a chair before the class and asked them to pray for me. The pain persisted, along with the frustration of not knowing how the forgiveness process could work for me.

Lorrie and I had needed to forgive each other for issues in our past that we had carried into our relationship. She seemed to forgive easily, but somehow I could not. Knowing that our relationship could easily end if I did not discover a way to let go of the past, I began to seek God for some answer, and He formed a process in my mind that finally worked and set me free from all of the unforgiveness I had carried for a lifetime.

My world did not become perfect overnight, and I was still occasionally hurt by something another person had said or done, but never again did it affect me long term. Since then, I have not allowed offense to find a lodging place in me or to stay around long enough to do me harm. The method of forgiveness I learned that day worked for me, and I have taught it to hundreds of couples over the years, who have also used it successfully.

What Will It Cost to Forgive?

The first question I ask when unforgiveness is present between a husband and wife is: "What will you have to give up to forgive?" Think about it. What will it cost you to forgive a person who has hurt you? The first thing you might have to give up is the hope that they will ever understand how very badly they hurt you. And you want them to know.

I often have the people I counsel write a letter of forgiveness, and in that letter they are to state the problem as clearly as they possibly can. The temptation is for them to leave that letter lying around somewhere that it can be found by the person in question. Some are tempted to leave it in a child's bag that will go home to that person or to let it be mailed to them "by mistake." Some are tempted to leave it in a prominent place on the hard drive of their computer and, to facilitate easy discover they will give it an unmistakable name. They may even take the time to highlight important parts of the letter in red or some other easily noticeable color in the hope of drawing the attention of the offending person.

What will it cost you to forgive a person who has hurt you?

Any and all of this type of activity probably indicates a wrong motive on our part. In forgiveness, we must relinquish, once and for all, the hope that those who have offended us will come to know how very much they have hurt us. That's no longer the point. The point is that we want to be free of bitterness and anger, and that's what forgiveness is all about.

The second thing you must give up when you forgive someone seems even worse to most people: You must give up the hope that the offending person or persons will ever have to pay for what they have done. But, although the mere thought of giving up all hope that the offending person will ever have to pay for their wrongs hurts you even more, it is a necessary part of forgiveness.

I asked one man whom I was counseling, "What do you want to see happen to her? Would you like to see her placed in stocks and publicly humiliated in the street? Would it help you somehow if she were lashed in the public square? Would it make you feel better to see her placed on a dunking stool? What is it that you want to see her go through? Should she be tarred and feathered and run out of town? If she walked barefoot on broken glass or through hot coals of fire, would it be enough to satisfy your aching heart? Should she be nailed to a cross?"

By asking this, I wasn't trying to minimize his pain in any way. That pain was genuine and very apparent. I was trying to get the man to realize what it means to forgive. When we do it, we relinquish all thoughts of vengeance, and this brings us freedom from the past. We leave to God the matter of punishment for our offenders.

The last thing we give up when we choose to forgive is the hope of somehow using the incident or incidents that have hurt us as a means of gaining advantage over the other party. In forgiveness, we suddenly allow the playing field to become leveled.

For instance, if we have been wronged in the marriage at some point and our partner is trying to hold us accountable at the moment, we could use the past as a tool and say, "After what you did to me, you want to hold *me* accountable?" This is a very commonly used tool, but forgiveness relinquishes this tool and agrees never to use it again. Then, suddenly, we are free to seriously work on making our relationship grow. Only by letting go of every stranglehold we can think of to use against each other can we hope to build something beautiful. Forgiveness repairs the foundation, and then it's ready for something serious and wonderful to be built upon it.

A true story is told of a king who punished murderers in the following way. He stripped both the murderer and his victim, and then had the dead body tied onto the killer back to back, so that skin touched skin. As the body of the dead man putrefied over the coming hours and days, it inevitably made the healthy man sick too, and he died as a result. A lot of people are carrying dead things around with them, and the results are disastrous.

When we forgive someone, they haven't won anything. We have won release from a sentence of certain death. Until we can forgive, we have a cadaver on our back, and it is infecting us, causing us bitterness, anger, resentment, and frustration. When enough of those violent toxins get built up inside of us, we are not fit to have a relationship with anyone. There is a wall a mile high separating us from others.

Very often the unforgiveness in us manifests itself as physical illness, and this can literally kill you. Holding bitterness in our hearts is clearly not worth the risks it entails.

One of the worst cases I ever had to deal with in this regard was that of a woman who had to admit to her husband that the child she was carrying in her womb was not his. That certainly would have to be the most painful pronouncement a husband could ever hear from his wife. However, in spite of deep pain and disappointment, he was able to forgive her, they agreed to keep the baby, and they went on to have a restored and fulfilling life together.

I would hate to think of how that particular situation would have worked out if the husband had not been willing or able to forgive. Their child would have been a daily reminder of the wrong committed against this husband, and it might have literally driven him insane.

After several years had gone by, we paid a visit to that family and were pleased to find them doing very well. The baby was no longer a baby, and although it was evident that he didn't look like the rest of the family, the husband had forgiven so fully and loved his wife so richly that none of what had happened mattered anymore.

Some couples are so bitter over things that have happened in the marriage that they barely speak to one another. How long could any relationship last under those circumstances? Get the marriage relationship right so that you can go on to develop other types of healthy relationships.

What the Bible Says About Forgiveness

The Bible has a lot to say about forgiveness. Let us briefly examine several relevant passages:

> *For if you forgive men when they sin against you, your heavenly Father will also forgive you. But if you do not forgive men their sins, your Father will not forgive your sins.* Matthew 6:14-15

This generic term *"men"* includes your spouse. If you are unwilling to forgive your spouse, then God is unwilling to forgive you. That places you outside the flow of God's grace, and I would not want to be in your position. It's not worth it.

> *Therefore, if you are offering your gift at the altar and there remember that your brother has something against you, leave your gift there in front of the altar. First go and be reconciled to your brother; then come and offer your gift.* Matthew 5:23-24

God cannot accept your gifts to Him and bless you financially if you have unforgiveness in your life. Is holding some grudge worth that risk?

And when you stand praying, if you hold anything against anyone, forgive him, so that your Father in heaven may forgive you your sins. Mark 11:25

God cannot hear your prayer (at least in the way you want Him to hear it) if you have unforgiveness in your heart. This is serious business.

Matthew 18 records a remarkable story known to Christians everywhere as the parable of the unmerciful servant. In this parable, there was a man called into account by his king because he owed him *"ten thousand talents,"* which was equivalent to many millions of dollars (Matthew 18:24). He was unable to pay, and so he and his wife and children were to be sold into slavery to satisfy the debt. The man fell on his knees and begged his master for mercy. If his master could be patient, he would repay the entire debt.

Moved by the man's plight, the king not only granted him his freedom; he completely canceled the large debt that had been owing. What a remarkable outcome!

If the story had ended there, it would be a happy one, but it didn't. This man, who had just been forgiven such a large debt, now went out and found one of his fellow servants who owed him *"a hundred denarii,"* which was equivalent to a few dollars (Matthew 18:28). Rather than show kindness, as had been done to him, he *"grabbed"* the man by the neck and *"began to choke him,"* demanding that the money be paid immediately (the same verse).

Amazingly, the reaction of this second servant was almost identical to the reaction of the first. He fell on his knees and begged for patience, assuring his creditor that if given a little time, he would repay the entire balance due. But this was not good enough for the first servant. Enraged, he ordered the second servant to be placed in jail until he could pay all of his debt.

It is not difficult to see why this angered the king when he heard about it. He immediately called for the servant. *"Shouldn't you have had mercy on your fellow servant just as I had on you?"* he asked (Matthew 18:33), and the answer was obvious.

Judgment was swift and decisive. The king reinstated the entire debt and had the man imprisoned until he could pay it all.

The story ended with these ominous words, recorded in the final verse of the chapter:

This is how my heavenly Father will treat each of you unless you forgive your brother [or sister] *from your heart.* Matthew 18:35

Who is the *"brother"* you need to forgive? It is your spouse, your wife or husband. If you can find it in your heart to forgive them, then your sin will be forgiven and forgotten. And if not, woe is you! God will not stand by and watch as any one of us mistreats one of His little ones.

There is a far more ominous implication to this story and its informative ending. If we have been forgiven, and we then fail to forgive others, our sins will be dredged up from the sea where they have been buried and again laid at our feet. What a horrible thought that is!

Unforgiveness isn't worth harboring, and if you don't learn to forgive your spouse, and your spouse doesn't learn to forgive you, your marriage will very likely not survive.

The Forgiveness Process

So what is the process that I used to break the bondage of unforgiveness in my life and which I have taught to many others? It combines two established and accepted methods of therapy: (1) letter writing and (2) the empty chair.

First, I have my clients write a five-part letter to the person they need to forgive. The first part of the letter is addressed to the offending party: "Dear Bill (Sam, Mary, Mom, Dad, etc.)." What is to follow requires you to literally go inside yourself and chip away all the painful memories and figuratively "vomit" them onto the pages you are writing. It thus becomes an accusatory letter that chronicles every event and instance of pain, anger, and embarrassment that you have experienced at the hands of the person who hurt you.

In writing such a letter, you can feel free to use any language you need to, as the person in question will never read it. That's not the purpose of your writing. This whole exercise is for you.

Don't allow time or fatigue to prevent you from listing down all the memories you have buried inside. And, since such memories have gone down into hiding with much emotion, bring them up with equal emotion. When this technique was revealed to me, I wrote a letter that was fully forty pages long—typewritten, double-spaced. Don't hesitate to get it all out into the open.

In the second part of the letter, you will say, "And now Bill (or whoever it was), I forgive you. I forgive you for _____." Then lump all of the items in Part I into categories and list them all again. As you do this, you don't have to feel the forgiveness; just mean what you're saying.

Part III continues the letter, but this time you address yourself. You need to forgive yourself. "And, now, Larry, I forgive you for carrying all of this pain around and allowing it to trash up your life all these years," or something similar (whatever fits your own circumstance, whatever you have had a hard time forgiving yourself for).

Part IV of the letter is written to God. "Heavenly Father, I ask that You forgive me. You told me in Your Word to forgive, and I haven't been able to do it until now. I ask for You to restore the flow of grace into my life and to make me whole again."

When we forgive, we will no longer be defined by the circumstances in our lives.

Finally, Part V of the letter requires the writer to finish this statement: "Now that I have forgiven and have been forgiven, my life will be different in the following ways: _____." What do I mean by this? Let me give you an example from the Bible.

The apostle John recorded the story of a man who had been sick for thirty-eight years and was waiting for someone to put him into the Pool of Bethesda so that he could be healed. Seeing him there in this condition, Jesus asked him a rather strange question: *"Do you want to get well?"* (John 5:6). I believe that Jesus was asking the man to inventory his heart, see what would be required of him if he were to be healed, and decide if he was willing to do it.

For instance, surely he would now have to get a job. He would have to rent a house and buy a donkey, as well as many other things. What's more, no one would ever again feel sorry for him, for he would no longer be a victim of his circumstances. Being healed would mean a huge change of lifestyle, but the man was willing, and so Jesus healed him.

When we forgive, we will no longer be defined by the circumstances in our lives. We will now be the person we have chosen to be rather than a victim of our past. That makes a huge difference.

When my clients come to their next session, I ask them how the letter writing went. After some discussion, I ask them to figuratively place the person they are forgiving in the chair in front of them and to read the letter to them as if they were really there. During this process, I turn my back to remove myself from the situation. After a few sentences, the pain begins to roll out, and often the client will cry from the pain or even scream at the person they are forgiving.

This is always a very emotional time, and after reading all the parts of their letter, the client is often ashen and spent. They have emptied themselves of all the pain.

At this point, I ask, "Are you willing to let it go and never reach for it again?" If the answer is yes, then I have them take the letter to my fireplace and burn it a page at a time and thus let it all go.

What a powerful process this has proven to be! The weight of all the bitterness and pain is lifted, and they are suddenly free of it. Why does it work so beautifully? Because forgiveness is God's idea, and He will never ask us to do something He has not equipped us for. In all the years I have used this method, I have never seen it fail even one time.

Some people forgive easily, but others do not. If you are trapped in your past by unforgiveness to your parents, an ex-spouse, your current spouse, or others, I recommend this process as a way to be set free.

4. Your Marriage Must Be Based on True Love

The fourth element that makes up a firm foundation for a successful marriage is a true and pure love. What do you really mean when you say the words "I love you"? Many people don't say these words nearly enough, but others say them and don't mean the right things.

All too often the answer I get when I ask the question is something like this: "It means I love how they love me, how they take care of me." "I love their warmth, their smile in the morning." This is not the answer I seek.

There is an old song called *I Love How You Love Me* by Bobby Vinton. It goes like this:

I love how your eyes close whenever you kiss me,
And when I'm away from you, I love how you miss me.
I love the way you always treat me tenderly.
But, darling, most of all I love how you love me.
I love how your heart beats whenever I hold you.
I love how you think of me without being told to.
I love the way your touch is always heavenly.
But, darling, most of all I love how you love me.

I love how your eyes close whenever you kiss me.
And when I'm away from you, I love how you miss me.
I love the way your touch is always heavenly.
But, darling, most of all I love how you love me.

I love how you hug me.
I love how you squeeze me, tease me, please me.
Love how you love me.
I love how you love me. [1]

I'm a romantic at heart, and I remember many old love songs. This one is flawed. Some of the words speak of true love, and others speak of appreciation for what someone does for us. As a foundation for marriage, we must love one another as an act that flows from us to them.

Love means that I will do things for Lorrie, whether or not she does things for me in return. This is especially so for us, men. In the Bible, five times God speaks to us to love our wives, and the word that is translated *"love"* in each of these five instances is *agape*, God's love. And when God tells us to love our wives, there are no ifs and no buts indicated. It is an unconditional love. *"Husbands, love your wives."* Period.

Husbands, love your wives, just as Christ loved the church and gave himself up for her. Ephesians 5:25

In this same way [as Christ loved the church], *husbands ought to love their wives as their own bodies. He who loves his wife loves himself.* Ephesians 5:28

Each one of you also must love his wife as he loves himself.... Ephesians 5:33

Husbands, love your wives and do not be harsh with them. Colossians 3:19

Several years ago, Lorrie and I were vacationing in Santa Rosa, California, and when I turned on the television one morning, a preacher was on. What I heard preached that day shook up my world.

"We men want our wives to wait on us hand and foot, don't we?" he said. "We sit down to watch a ball game, and we want them to bring us something to eat. Then we want some ice cream, and we expect them to serve it to us. Next, we want to top it all off with some coffee, and we expect that to be served to us as well. If, for some reason, our wives are not serving us as we expect them to, we wonder what's wrong with them."

He went on to point out that the model given to us in the Bible was Christ and His relationship with His bride, and in this relationship, Jesus did not sit on a throne and expect to be served hand and foot. Rather than call on everyone to heed His every beck and call, He was the one to don the towel and wash His disciples' feet. This fact shocked them then, and somehow it still seems shocking to us men in the twenty-first century that we are called to serve our bride.

Somewhere along the line things have gotten turned on their head, and we now have it all backward. We expect to be served, when we are called to serve.

Jesus taught us what to do if we want to become great:

The greatest among you will be your servant. Matthew 23:11

Whoever wants to become great among you must be your servant, and whoever wants to be first must be slave of all. For even the Son of Man did not come to be served, but to serve.... Mark 10:43-45

To many, that would seem to be an upside down kind of leadership, but Jesus said that the first would be last and the last first (see Matthew 19:30). Paul taught that it is in our weakness that we truly become strong (see 2 Corinthians 12:10).

Men, the wonderful thirteenth chapter of Paul's first letter to the Corinthians has our names all over it. Listen to God's heart:

Love is patient, love is kind. It does not envy, it does not boast, it is not proud. It is not rude, it is not self-seeking, it is not easily angered, it keeps no record of wrongs. Love does not delight in evil but rejoices with the truth. It always protects, always trusts, always hopes, always perseveres. Love never fails.... And now these three remain: faith, hope and love. But the greatest of these is love. 1 Corinthians 13:4-8, 13

How have you been doing in applying this kind of love to your relationship with your wife? Are you patient with her? Are you kind to her?

Or are you envious of her? Are you boastful to her? Are you proud before her? Are you rude to her? Are you self-seeking with her? Are you easily angered with her? Do you keep a record of wrongs she has done to you?

Do you always protect, always trust, always hope, and always persevere? That's what it should mean when you tell her, "I love you."

It is foolish to think about building any other part of the marriage house if this foundation piece is missing or damaged. Forget the floor plan for now. Forget what the rooms will look like and how each one will be furnished. It would be foolhardy to try to dress up something that is about ready to collapse. Get this foundational piece in place, and then you will be ready to go on to other issues.

By addressing the men first, I don't mean to be freeing the women from this requirement of true love. Paul, in writing to Titus, suggested that wives may need to be taught to love their husbands, just as husbands are instructed to love their wives (see Titus 2:4). It's just that we men were called first to this duty by our Maker.

Again, when God called us to love our wives as He loves the Church and gave Himself for it, there are no conditional clauses, no ifs. He didn't say, "If she is lovable, love her in return." We are to love her—regardless of the circumstances.

What did the Lord mean when He mentioned that we should love our wives as He loved the Church *"and gave Himself for it"*? Does that mean that we should die for our wives? It means that we should do anything that she needs us to do, that we should be willing to do whatever is necessary to provide for her and protect her.

One man said to his wife, "I would die for you, Baby."

She responded, "I don't need you to die; I just need you to help me do the dishes."

One man was reminding his wife of the beautiful picture painted by Proverbs 31 of a woman so endowed by God's favor that she blesses her family and her community on every hand. Of particular interest to him were the lines:

She gets up while it is still dark; she provides food for her family. Proverbs 31:15

"I'd like some hot cereal," he told her.

But this man had not inspired his wife as the man behind the woman of Proverbs 31 had. This woman's response was, "Well, if you want hot cereal, then set your corn flakes on fire."

Get it right, men. True love makes all the difference in the world.

...respect is earned over time through the consistent demonstration of love.

Love is patient, love is kind.

Have you been patient with your wife over the past few days? Have you been kind to her? When she made a mistake (and we all make them), did you chew her out royally and act condescending toward her?

Somehow we have the idea that we can just dish out the orders for the entire family, and everyone must scurry about trying to obey our every whim. But respect is earned over time through the consistent demonstration of love.

Many men are public successes, but in private (in the home) they are failures. And their area of failure is serious, for it is in the highest of their callings, that of a faithful and loving husband and father. Men, let us abandon hypocrisy and seek to perform well our God-given calling as husband and father. Let us live what we preach and teach. Let us walk the talk.

Start working as hard on your marriage as you do on your job. Start treating your family with as much, or more, respect as you do your professional colleagues.

Stop criticizing each other, stop being disrespectful to each other in public (and in private), and stop speaking rudely to each other anywhere and everywhere. Maybe what is coming out of your mouth is just normal, just what's inside of you. But if so, ask God to change that. Pray as David did:

Create in me a pure heart, O God, and renew a steadfast [right] *spirit within me.* Psalm 51:10

The Bible says much about the heart of man and its need for reform:

The heart is deceitful above all things and beyond cure. Who can understand it? Jeremiah 17:9

The *King James Version* of the Bible says that the heart is *"desperately wicked."*

Above all else, guard your heart, for it is the wellspring of life. Proverbs 4:23

The *King James Version* renders these final words as: *"Out of it are the issues of life."*

David sang:

I have hidden your word in my heart that I might not sin against you. Psalm 119:11

Jesus said:

For out of the heart come evil thoughts, murder, adultery, sexual immorality, theft, false testimony, slander. Matthew 15:19

Are any of these things coming out of your mouth? If you are calling each other names (and I've had Spirit-filled believers do it to each other in my presence), you're out of line. Such conduct has no place in a marriage, especially in a Christian marriage.

Love is not self-seeking. It is not selfish. It is not easily angered.

One day, not long ago, Lorrie did or said something that angered me. I can't even remember what it was now, and that's usually how it is. But I do remember that it happened very quickly and that I was very angry. Then a wonderful thing happened. The Holy Spirit spoke to my heart and said, *"Love is not easily angered."* I felt in that moment that I had reached a milestone in our relationship. I was not proud of the fact that I had gotten angry with Lorrie, but I was proud of the fact that I was hearing from God on the subject.

The Scriptures teach us:

Everyone should be quick to listen, slow to speak and slow to become angry.
James 1:19

Wow! How about that? How is it that we have taken what the Bible calls sin (impatience, unkindness, rudeness, etc.) and tried to make it acceptable? It's not acceptable, not at all.

Love keeps no record of wrongs.

Once you have forgiven, you cannot keep a list of grievances—what she did and what she didn't do or what he did and what he didn't do.

Love does not delight in evil but it rejoices with the truth.

It [love] always protects, always trusts, always hopes, always perseveres.

Today, in the twenty-first century, we are hesitant to say "always" about anything, but the Bible doesn't hesitate. It boldly declares, *"ALWAYS."* We mortals can't seem to say always about anything, but here the Bible says always about everything.

Love never fails to protect. It never fails to trust. It never fails to hope for the future. It never fails to persevere. It keeps going—no matter what.

Love is like the Ever-Ready Bunny. It keeps going and going—even when it encounters obstacles.

Love never fails.

If I didn't say another thing in this book, this would be worth the price of it. Love is more than words, and when you say, "I love you," there has to be something behind those words.

Every time you say "I love you," you are saying:

I will be patient with you.

I will be kind to you.

I will not envy you.

I will not boast against you.

I will not be proud against you.

I will not be rude with you.

I will not be self-seeking with you.

I will not be easily angered with you.

I will not keep any record of wrongs you have done.

I will not delight in evil against you, but I will rejoice in the truth.

I will always protect you.

I will always trust you.

I will always have hope for our future together.

I will always persevere. No matter what comes, I will not give up.

And if that's not what you're saying, then don't say the words and not mean them. Let your marriage be founded upon true love.

5. Your Marriage Must Be Based on True Friendship

The final element that makes up a firm foundation for a successful marriage is true friendship. Your spouse must become your best friend, and you must become your spouse's best friend.

It seems utterly impossible to believe, but many people marry without ever becoming good friends. I couldn't believe what I was hearing when I was told by one couple I counseled that the man had sold his wife a car. What happened to *"they will become one flesh"* (Genesis 2:24)?

"That's mine," some spouses say, "leave it alone," but in marriage, there is no "yours" or "mine." What does it mean when a husband says, "I bought my wife a car," but it turns out that she is making the payments on it?

Some spouses keep separate checking accounts. He spends his money the way he wants, and she spends her money the way she wants. One couple said to me, "That works for us."

"Well," I challenged, "I would be willing to bet that I can have the two of you in an argument over money before you leave this office tonight." And it happened. They were screaming at each other. It came to that because he was trying to set aside money for retirement, and she wasn't helping him with it, and she was saying it was time to buy the children's school clothes, and he wasn't helping her with that.

When you become one through marriage, you then hold all things in common. That is the highest form of friendship.

Many couples live like they are still single, each having their own circle of friends. You must develop a friendship with each other and mutual interests, or your marriage will not be fulfilling.

When you become one through marriage, you then hold all things in common.

What exactly does it mean to be *"one flesh"*? What did God have in mind when He joined two very different individuals together? Did He intend for them to remain strangers to each other? Certainly not.

In order to form this new one-flesh relationship, He required that there be a breaking of other long-standing, close-knit ties. He said:

> *For this reason a man will leave his father and mother and be united to his wife, and they will become one flesh.* Genesis 2:24

Normally, our tie to mother and father is the most natural and the first to be formed in each of our lives. But when we marry, a new relationship is formed that is to take precedence over even that natural birth tie. In marriage, our best friends cannot be Dad and Mom, or else we're in trouble.

When any spouse goes running to Dad and Mom at the first sign of trouble in the marriage, it's a mistake. Some spouses are joined to each other physically, but they are still joined to others emotionally.

God hasn't called spouses to go back and live with their parents. He told them to *"leave"* father and mother. That's severance. And He told them to *"cleave"* (KJV) or *"be united"* to their spouse. That's permanence. That's just like muscle clinging to bone. You can hardly get it off. When you *"cleave"* to your wife, you're stuck together, and nothing can separate you. The two of you are one flesh. That's the unity we are to experience in marriage.

The Scriptures go on to say:

The man and his wife were both naked, and they felt no shame. Genesis 2:25

That is the intimacy that we are to share in the bond of marriage.

But what happens to us? Why are so many not becoming good friends? In most cases, it's because couples are having sex before marriage. They are not taking time to get to know each other before they become sexually intimate. It takes time to build a friendship, and most are not willing to wait that long. They want to jump right into bed together, and they end up having sex with a stranger.

Many can't go for a simple walk around the park without thinking about where this will eventually lead them. Consequently, many never make it out of the park. They become intimate right there. And what have they done? They have skipped friendship and jumped right into sexual intimacy, and when they come to a marriage counselor like me, we have to discover and inform them that they have never truly become friends. This discovery doesn't take long; it is rather obvious.

Friendship formed before marriage is then something we can fall back on when hard times come. If such a friendship has never been formed, what can we do then? The only solution is then to go back and form the friendship that should have been formed long ago.

Additionally, when we carry sexual baggage into the marriage, it complicates everything.

Six Areas of Intimacy in Your Relationship

Part of forming a true friendship in marriage consists of examining areas of intimacy in your relationship. There are six important areas that I want to touch very briefly:

A. Intellectual Intimacy

This is a mutual regard that we must have for the thoughts and opinions of each other. When your wife comes up with a great idea and you put her down, you have destroyed intellectual intimacy. Often I hear troubled couples saying, "If somebody else says it, she'll listen, but if I say it, she won't." And this goes for husbands as well.

I respect what Lorrie says, and I give it equal credence. After all, we're part of the same union, two adults of equal intelligence. I can't afford to put down her thoughts, and she can't afford to put down my thoughts. My thoughts have value, and so do hers.

B. Social Intimacy

In his book *The Drifting Marriage*, Donald Harvey[2] names three areas of life: crisis, calm, and "hecticness." The crises are often what draw us together, but it is during calm times that we build our relationship. What he called "hecticness," meaning the busyness of life, beats us to death because we get so busy that we only have time for formalities:

"Good morning, Dear. Did you sleep well?"

"Yes."

"See you after work."

"Bye, Honey."

"Hi, Honey, I'm home."

"Did you have a good day?"

"Yes."

"Good night, Dear. Sleep well."

"Thank you, and you too."

This is a politeness we might use with any coworker or friend, not with our very best friend and lover. The friendship of marriage must go much deeper than that.

Some people say to me, "It doesn't do us any good to go out to eat together because when we do we have nothing to talk about." Others go out to eat together, and all they talk about is the children, money matters, and their work.

What exactly should couples be talking about when they are alone? They should be talking about their dreams, their goals, and their hopes, where they want to go together in life.

Enjoying social intimacy in the marriage doesn't mean that you cannot have other friends, but don't have so many friends that you forget what it's like to be alone together and enjoy each other. If you always have dinner with friends, always take vacations with friends, and always do your recreation with friends, how can the marriage be strengthened and grow? You have left no room for intimacy. Don't allow the hectic pace of life to chew you up and spit you out.

C. Recreational Intimacy

Just because you got married doesn't mean that you must stop having fun. In fact, if you do stop having fun, you will do grave harm to the marriage. Play with each other. Act like kids again. Don't be so serious. Life was meant for enjoyment.

This calls for a little joke: A lady had a near death experience, and God told her to go back and that she could live another twenty-seven years, eleven days, and two and a half hours. She was so happy with her new lease on life that she decided to make some major changes. She had a face lift, liposuction, and some reconstructive surgery, and she looked and felt like a new woman.

Two weeks later, she was hit by a car and killed. When she got to heaven, she couldn't wait to question God. "I thought You said that I would have another twenty-seven years, eleven days, and two and a half hours to live?"

"Whoops!" God said. "I didn't recognize you."

Lighten up and enjoy life.

D. Emotional Intimacy

Emotional intimacy is the connectedness you feel when the two of you are together, and it is the glue that holds your marriage together.

E. Spiritual Intimacy

A man and a woman who join themselves in the flesh and become one in that way owe it to themselves to talk together about their relationship with God. We need to talk at a deep level with our spouse about who God is to us and what He is saying to us and revealing to us through His Word in our private times with Him. This creates a spiritual intimacy.

F. Sexual Intimacy

The Bible is full of instructions about sexual intimacy, and this must become a normal and healthy part of every caring relationship. We will, of course, deal with this subject more in detail in subsequent chapters.

How Can You Build a More Intimate Friendship?

There are many things you can do to develop a more intimate friendship. One of them is to have a regular date night each week. And, yes, this can be done even if you have small children.

Don't take your children with you that particular night, don't take your parents with you, and don't take your friends with you. Go alone.

I once saw an interesting three-frame cartoon. In the first frame, the husband and wife were sitting in a restaurant with their hands joined across the table staring intently at each other. The caption read, "Isn't it great that the kids are away?"

In the second frame, he is looking out one window, and she is looking out another one.

In the third frame, they turn to each other and say, "So, when will the kids be back?"

This man and wife, like many, were so wrapped up in their children that they had forgotten how to enjoy each other. This is a deadly mistake. Have a night out together, and agree ahead of time that your night out is for enjoyment, not for any serious discussion of problems.

Aside from your night out, spend time during the week talking to each other. According to experts in this field, you should have at least fifteen hours of conversation each week. That's more than two hours each day. How can you have a relationship if you're not talking?

You don't have time for it? You'd better find time if you want to make your marriage a success.

Find ways to have fun together.

Pray together. This not only builds intimacy, but it strengthens you spiritually and brings God's blessing into your life. Lorrie and I did not pray together for the first several years of our marriage. Then, when times got tough as parents, we felt the need to join our faith together and begin to pray with each other. Now, we pray together twice a day—once in the morning and then again just before we go to sleep at night. Jesus declared:

> *Again, I tell you that if two of you on earth agree about anything you ask for, it will be done for you by my Father in heaven.* Matthew 18:19

There is power in agreement.

Taking Inventory

It never hurts to pause and take inventory of your life, and the same is true for your marriage. Now that you know what acceptable foundations for any successful marriage are, check to see if you have them in place:

- Are you in covenant with each other? Have you made an unfailing commitment to each other's future?

- Do you trust each other? "Trust her?" "Trust him?" Yes, it's a requirement for a sound marriage.

- Are you holding on to any unforgiveness? If you are, it's time for you to let it go.

- Do you really love each other? If so, you now know what you have to do.

- Do you have a deep and abiding friendship? If not, it's time to work on that.

When all is said and done, each of us will be held accountable individually by God. Lorrie will not be able to answer for me on that day, and I will not be able to answer for her. Men, you have been given by God the awesome responsibility of being the head of your household, the spiritual leader of your wife and children. I hope you appreciate the gravity of that responsibility.

Many of us are overwhelmed by all that life has thrown our way. We have so many problems at work and with friends that it seems very difficult for us to have the time and spiritual energy required to dedicate to making our marriage and family all that it should be. But if we can get this right, then everything else in life will fall into place. Conversely, if we get everything else right and fail at this one thing, we will have failed at the most important part of our life—second only to our relationship with God.

Men, it's worth the effort to strengthen the marriage. God designed it to be something wonderful, and you owe it to yourself to work toward His plan.

Stop blaming each other for the problems you face, and start looking inside yourself. Ask God what it is that He wants you to do to better your marriage.

Ladies, you can't just blame your husband for the failures in your relationship. God has given you the responsibility to follow His instruction manual to build a foundation for a marriage that will go the distance. It's worth the dedication of any time and effort this may require.

Both of you need to change, to put yourselves into alignment with God's Word. Someone said that the definition of *crazy* is figuring out what doesn't work and continuing to do it. Another definition of *crazy* is to keep doing what you are presently doing and expect a different result. You will have to make some changes if you expect to make your marriage all that God meant it to be. ⬿

Identifying Needs in the Relationship and Learning How to Meet Them

(Or How to Affair-Proof Your Marriage and Provide Mutual Contentment)

If any man desire to be first, the same shall be last of all, and servant of all. Mark 9:35 KJV

It would be great to be part of a relationship in which each partner automatically understood the needs of the other and responded to them, because meeting each other's needs is the very best way to achieve mutual contentment in the relationship. Since that rarely happens, we have to teach each other about our needs. Before we get into specific needs, let us take a look at what we really mean by needs.

What Are Needs? And Why Are They Important?

There is a difference between a need and a want. A need is nonnegotiable; it must be met. You simply cannot negotiate it away. It's like air, water, and food to your physical body. If you don't have them, you will shut down and eventually die. In the same way, there are emotional needs that are critical. They must be met, and if any partner does not have their needs met in the relationship, they will feel forced to go elsewhere (if they are not in a covenant relationship).

Meeting the needs of my mate, then, is a responsibility that I cannot shirk. If Lorrie were drowning and I had a life preserver that I could throw to her to save her life, and yet I said, "I think I'm too tired to do this, and, besides, I don't feel very well right now," I would be selfishly putting her life at risk. Emotional needs are just that critical; we must have them met, or we will die—emotionally.

...there are emotional needs that are critical.

Wants can be negotiated. "I'll give you a back rub, if you'll rub my aching feet." If a spouse is too tired to respond to this, their mate won't necessarily die. A back rub is like icing on the cake, but needs are what one must have from the relationship.

As a therapist, I'm the last stop on the railroad, and by the time couples come to me, their situation is usually critical. Most of those who come to me have the same story: their needs are no longer being met in the relationship. When I can get that couple to the place that one or more of the partners feel that their needs are again being met, I know that I'm on the road to a successful healing of the relationship.

To many, speaking about personal needs may sound very selfish, almost narcissistic, but it is quite biblical. Jesus said to us, His bride:

If you love me, you will obey what I command. John 14:15

Paul wrote to the believers of the first century:

Husbands, love your wives, just as Christ loved the church and gave himself up for her. Ephesians 5:25

As Christians, our model for marriage is Christ and the Church and the wonderful relationship they enjoy. Christ gave Himself for the needs of His Bride.

If I love Lorrie, I will love her the way she needs me to love her, and if Lorrie loves me, she will love me the way I need her to love me. That is what marriage is all about, and if a marriage is anything less than that, it may not last very long.

Jesus didn't ask us to show our love for Him by walking barefooted on hot coals or broken glass. He didn't ask us to be nailed to a cross. The Word declares:

Does the Lord delight in burnt offerings and sacrifices as much as in obeying the voice of the Lord? 1 Samuel 15:22

Our obedience to Christ reveals our love for Him. This concept was taken a step further in John's first letter to the churches:

We know that we have come to know him if we obey his commands. The man who says, "I know him," but does not do what he commands is a liar, and the truth is not in him. But if anyone obeys his word, God's love is truly made complete in him.... Whoever claims to live in him must walk as Jesus did. 1 John 2:3-6

These are Christ's words to His bride, and it is a model that we can use for our own marriage. If we are unwilling to show love to a mate in the way they have taught us they need to be loved, then we don't really love them.

The words "I love you" can be just that—words. If you say the words, and you don't back them up with deeds, then the words are empty. They're essentially a lie.

I need to love my wife in the way she has taught me, and she needs to love me in the way I have taught her. Anything else is something short of a relationship that is mutually satisfying.

How Do I Determine My Needs?

So what are my needs? How do I determine what exactly they are? We know up front that there are not many of them—just a few things that we absolutely cannot live without. The rest are wants that are negotiable. But what are the criteria for determining actual needs? There are three:

1. What do you do for other people and then you get angry or hurt if they don't do it back to you?

"Why do you do that?" someone might ask us. Usually the answer is because it's what we would like someone to do for us in return. If we need to hear someone say, "I love you," we say "I love you." If we need sex, we offer sexual intimacy. If we need communication, we talk a lot. If we need touch, then we touch others. We give out naturally what we interpret as love, and it is usually what we expect and need in return.

The problem comes when you try to give to your spouse what you interpret as love, and it doesn't seem like love to them. It feels so good to you, but it doesn't feel nearly as good to them. You love to be touched, but they don't like to be touched as much. "Why are you always touching me?" they complain.

You love to hear the words, "I love you," so you say it a lot, but after a while your spouse responds irritably, "I love you! I love you! I love you! Okay, I got it. If it changes at some point, let me know." But if your mate needs to hear you say the words, then you need to learn to say the words.

Scott Peck in his book *The Road Less Traveled* [3] says that love is the discipline to continue doing in marriage what we did out of passion during courtship. We did it well then, and we must do it well now. If you opened the door for her and were otherwise attentive to her needs then, how much more you should do that now. If you were Don Juan then, you need to be Don Juan now and not Don Juan asleep.

Some men act like they're coming home from the hunt. They have their prey all bagged and slung over their shoulder, and they think they can relax now. Marriage all too often spells the end of courtship and chivalry, and we gradually stop doing the things we did out of the passion of courtship.

If a spouse has stopped being the warm and wonderful person you thought they were, what can you do? If you are not the warm and wonderful person you were in courtship, what can you do? This is when the discipline of the responsibility of marriage kicks in. I am responsible to meet my spouse's needs, so I must learn what they are and how I can best respond to them. There is no acceptable alternative.

Early in our marriage Lorrie taught me how she wanted to be loved, and I wrote that on the back of my eyelids so that every time I close my eyes I see it. Basically, needs never change. The intensity may need to change at some point, but not the need itself.

At one point, about five years into our marriage, Lorrie decided that her needs must have changed. "After all, she said, I never get angry about this and this and this anymore."

"Did it ever occur to you," I said rather smugly, "that just maybe I am doing such a great job of meeting your needs that you don't even think about them anymore?" Boy, did I have to eat those words!

When we had that conversation it was Christmastime. On New Year's Eve Lorrie and I went to a church party. We were playing Trivial Pursuit as couples, and when I knew the answer to several questions, I just blurted them out without first consulting her.

At the time, that seemed perfectly acceptable to me. After all, I already knew the answer. Why should I seek her help? But what I didn't realize at the moment was that my actions were very hurtful to her. She needed to feel important to me, and I wasn't doing anything to make her feel important.

Before long, I put my hand on her leg and was surprised to find that it was cold—very cold—icy cold. All the warmth had somehow gone out of her.

I made another mistake that night. I got up and went walking around taking photos of those attending the event and left Lorrie unattended. It didn't take long to discover the problem. When a need isn't being met, that becomes quickly apparent.

Each of us has the obligation to teach our mates what pleases us, what is important to us, what we need, and also to ask them what pleases them, what is important to them, what they need.

2. What do you fight about and are never able to resolve?

There may be something that bothered you in a previous relationship, and you were never able to come to any agreement on it. Or, there may well be something that bothers you about your current relationship. Do you fight about sex and never resolve the issue? Then one or the other party is not having their needs met in this area. Do you fight about money and cannot find resolution? If so, then one or the other party has a need that is not being met in this area. Do you fight about the children? If so, one or the other party has a need that is being buried in the confusion of child raising.

Whatever you fight about and cannot resolve represents a need on someone's part that is not being met. That must be addressed, or the consequences could be fatal.

3. What is so important to you that it could cause you to leave the relationship if you didn't have it?

You know yourself better than anyone else knows you, and you know what you need. Is there something that would shut you down and cause you to leave the relationship? If so, that is a need that must be addressed.

> *Whatever you fight about and cannot resolve represents a need on someone's part that is not being met.*

When I was speaking at a fairly large church once there was a man sitting on the very last bench at the back. I could tell that he wasn't happy with the idea of needs as I was presenting it. I said to the group, "What, for instance, if Lorrie said to me, 'Let's just be good friends. We can grow old together, but I never want to have anything to do with you sexually again'?"

I heard him mutter, "That's not fair!" and I knew that I had him. I usually know how to get to men on this subject of needs, because sex is a big part of most men's needs. Most men could not imagine their wives telling them such a thing. That would shut them down and cause them to look elsewhere.

But sex is just one need. There are others, and they are just as important as sex. Men who are in a covenant relationship would not necessarily leave their wives and seek intimacy with other women, but at the very least they would shut down emotionally and become withdrawn.

Lorrie has committed herself never to withhold herself from me sexually because she knows my need in this area. When we first discussed it years ago, she said to me, "What if I became a quadriplegic and could no longer meet your need?"

It was a legitimate question, and it required a thoughtful answer, so I pondered long before responding. In the end, I felt that this would be a very different situation. If she were withholding her love willingly, that would be one thing, but to be unable to respond would be something else entirely. I could live with that. My brain can handle "I can't," but it cannot handle "I won't." Needs run deep and are powerful forces within any relationship. If you ignore them, you will suffer the consequences.

The Basic Needs of Men and the Basic Needs of Women

Some needs are not gender specific, but many are, and there are some needs that seem to be common to most men. Not every man has every single one of them, but most will have a majority of them. Learn to identify your specific needs by applying the three criteria above.

- With most men, the sexual need ranks very high on the list.

- Men need to be admired and respected by their wives.

- Men need a neat and orderly house to come home to.

- Men need to feel like they have an attractive spouse.

- Men need recreational companionship (only occasionally do they want to go out alone).

Some people do need time alone, and I can say that by experience. Early in our marriage Lorrie and I were in Maui, Hawaii, staying at the beautiful and romantic Maui Marriott, and one evening Lorrie quite unexpectedly said to me, "I need to have the evening to myself."

I was shocked and incredulous. "What? We're in this wonderfully romantic place, and you want to be alone?" I was devastated. She must not love me like I thought she did.

When I get frustrated or angry, I look for something to do around the house, some housework, and then I go storming around, banging things more than is called for, and in this way I work off my frustration. But that night there was no housework to be done.

There was a small laundromat in the hotel, so I proceeded to gather up all of our dirty clothes and took them to the laundromat. Then, while the clothes went through the wash and dry cycles, I stomped up and down the beach trying to figure out what was going on in our marriage. I simply could not understand Lorrie's need to be alone.

My mistake was taking it all very personally. As it turned out, Lorrie wasn't trying to get away from me; she needed to be away from everyone and everything. She needed time alone with the Lord to recharge her batteries. In time I learned to understand and accept this need, and her occasional desire to be alone no longer bothered me. Until I was able to understand it, I interpreted her actions as rejection of me, and that hurt.

We have occasionally hosted tours to Israel, some cruises, conferences, and our marriage seminars, and I always know that about halfway through any of them Lorrie will inevitably disappear for a day. In fact, I suggest it now as a way of showing my care for her and honoring her need to be alone sometimes.

What do women need?

- Women need to feel like they're number one in their husband's life, the most important, cherished and treasured person on earth to him.

- Women need their husbands to be their spiritual companion and leader. (This fact can scare men to death until they come to understand what it really means.)

- Women need their husbands to be honest and open, and many times men are neither.

- Women need their husbands to communicate with them. (Studies have shown that men speak some twelve thousand words a day, and women speak at least twice that much. Lorrie says it's because our women always have to tell us something twice before we finally understand. By the time most men get home from work, they have run out of words, but they need to find some more because the need of their wives to communicate must be met.)

- Women need nonsexual affection. (Most men find this hard to understand. To them, a romantic evening always ends with physical lovemaking, but that is not necessarily true for the wife.)

- Women need financial security. (They need to know that there's enough money coming in to pay the bills, that they're not about to be put out on the street. They're disturbed by late notices and the thought of someone coming to repossess the car. They need to know that the husband they trust to lead them is making appropriate decisions about their financial future.)

These are needs, men, so they are nonnegotiable.

Knowing the basic needs of men and of women, is it any wonder that the Bible says to wives: *"The wife must respect her husband"* (Ephesians 5:33), and to husbands: *"Husbands, love your wives just as Christ loved the church and gave himself up for her"* (Ephesians 5:25)? God knows well the creature He formed from the dust, and He knows what we need. It is time that we discover these things as well.

The Greatest Need of Men

As stated earlier, the greatest need often expressed by men is for sex. But if I need sex, I must express that to my spouse. How else will she know that the need exists? Since I am the one with the need, it is my responsibility to teach my spouse how to fulfill it.

With most men, the sexual issue that is most often a cause of conflict is the frequency of sex. How often should we make love? When I ask men, they often give me a range of possibilities. "Once or twice a week," "two or three times a week," "three or four times a month" are all common answers. I can usually know that the low number is given to gain the woman's acceptance, but the higher number is really the husband's desire. So, women, go with the higher number if you want to be safe.

If meeting your husband's sexual need means that you have to keep track with a calendar how many times you are making love, then that's what you need to do. This is important and cannot be overlooked, and the same is true for other needs. A spouse's need cannot be shunted aside for other important matters.

Sometimes the roles are reversed, and it is the woman who has the need for more sexual intimacy and not the man.

Some spouses don't want to be the one to initiate sex or at least not to *always* be the one to initiate sex. Talk this over, and come to some agreement about it. Each person needs to feel desired, and men need to feel desired just as women do. You may agree to share the initiation 55 or some other percentage.

Ladies, the fact that your husband desires you sexually is the highest compliment he could possibly pay you. It may not feel that way to you at the time, but accept it as such. Because sex is so important to him, he is telling you that he wants you to share the most important part of his life.

Both spouses need to be open to sexual experimentation. The term "missionary position," in which spouses make love face to face with the man on top, got it's name because missionaries went all over the world telling people that this was the only acceptable way to make love. In this way, they sowed a lot of confusion. He might need you to be open to doing something different so that your sexual relationship never becomes mechanical.

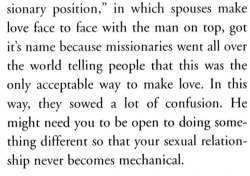

Men, don't be hesitant to tell your wife when you have needs.

Experiment with touching and stroking so that you can find places on your spouse's body, other than the fairly well-known erogenous zones, that are sensitive and use them to bring your spouse pleasure.

He may need you to be willing to make love in a variety of settings. Put on some sensual clothing or sleep in the nude occasionally. Do whatever you need to do to keep your relationship fresh and glowing. Take some action to meet the need of the moment.

Men, don't be hesitant to tell your wife when you have needs. My personal opinion is that if you have been in a relationship before and you know what your sexual needs are, you should make these known to your spouse even before marriage. That way there can be no doubts and no second guessing later. Understand each other's needs, and be sure you are willing to meet them before you are joined as husband and wife.

Some people insist that they will not participate in any sexual experimentation, but I am referring to experimentation that is safe, not prohibited in the Bible, offensive or harmful. Why not learn something new? What could it possibly hurt? You never know; you might even enjoy it.

Set up an occasional romantic or sexual encounter away from home. Plan a romantic weekend getaway on an anniversary or some other special occasion. Either of you can initiate this.

Don't be guilty of pushing your partner away when they touch you in a suggestive way, look at you in a suggestive way, or speak to you in a suggestive way. If there are good reasons for postponing or denying sexual pleasures, those need to be presented in the most tactful way, so as not to hurt your spouse's ego. The Scriptures teach:

> *Do not deprive each other except by mutual consent and for a time, so that you may devote yourselves to prayer. Then come together again so that Satan will not tempt you because of your lack of self-control.* 1 Corinthians 7:5

As clear as some scriptures are, we should not be guilty of using the Bible as a weapon against each other. This is not its purpose. Use the Word of God only to challenge each other to higher heights. It shows God's plan for your ultimate happiness.

Reading and discussing good books about marriage will build a stronger, healthier marriage. *His Needs, Her Needs* by Willard Harley[4] is a great example, but others are mentioned throughout this book and in the bibliography that appears at the end. *His Needs, Her Needs* was a source for some of the topics covered in this chapter.

The Greatest Need of Women

Probably 95 percent of the women who have come to me for counseling, the women who have been in my seminars, and even my own wife have stated their greatest need as being number one in their husband's life. Men are often inept at showing their woman that she is the most important person in the world to them.

If we fix a glass of orange juice and bring it to her in bed, and she doesn't even like orange juice, what does that prove? If we buy her certain flowers because we like that kind of flowers, what does that prove? We might change the oil filter on her car and think we're doing something great, but to her that may not be something great at all. We need to learn what really pleases her and then do it.

One thing I hear often is that women love it when we walk close to them. That's very important to them. Even with couples who go to church together, the men are often out of the car and halfway to the door of the church before the wife can get the children out of the car. To some women, this may not be a big thing, but if it is, he needs to learn how to make her feel important.

One way to be certain you are always walking side-by-side is to embrace each other, either having your arm around each other or holding hands. How can you do that and be many paces apart? Lorrie helped me to realize how important this issue was to her.

When you are walking down the street, it is important to some women that her man is walking on the outside, next to the street. This gives her a greater sense of security. The fact that he is willing to do this for her shows her that he indeed treasures her.

Opening the door for her is another way we can show her how important she is. When we were first married, I would get out of the car and start to turn toward wherever we were going. Then, when I realized that Lorrie was not with me, I would turn to see where she was. To my surprise, she was still seated in the car waiting for me to come around and open the door for her. That didn't prove to be a need that she could never live without, but it was an action step that could show her my love. It made her feel important and special.

Buying cards or flowers on special occasions may be important—our anniversary, her birthday. She loves to give cards, and she loves to receive them too. It's important to her.

She loves to give flowers on special occasions, and she loves to receive them too.

Lorrie needs me to do a special "I love you" once a month as an action step to her need to feel number one to me. This means that I do something for her that I didn't *have* to do. There is no special occasion; I just create a special occasion. I might be traveling and see some small item I want her to have or I know she would love, so I buy it for her. I call her when I don't need to call her. I do something for her that is unexpected and without obligation.

At one of our retreats, we were doing a newlywed game, and one of the questions asked first to our spouses was: "What's the most romantic thing your husband has done for you lately?" My mind raced as I tried to think what Lorrie would say. Which "I love you" would she choose? I made a couple of guesses, but she said no to each of them. When her answer came, I was both surprised and pleased.

"It was the other night when I was so cold in bed and you put the blow dryer under the sheets to warm my feet up," she said. "That was a most romantic thing to me, and it didn't even cost you anything. But it surely did make me feel treasured, loved, and important to you."

It is important to Lorrie that I include her in social settings. If someone approaches us, I need to introduce her and draw her into the conversation. For one thing, she needs to know that I'm very proud to introduce her as my wife.

A very good way to show your devotion to your wife may be to write her a love note at least once a month.

What pleases a woman may be that we defer to her before other family members or friends. Her desires should always take precedence. "Mama invited us for Thanksgiving, but what would you like to do?" She may want to begin a whole new family tradition at your house.

A very good way to show your devotion to your wife may be to write her a love note at least once a month. For some this may be very difficult, while others can wax eloquent without much effort.

Another way is to call her at least once a day from work. If you have to tie a string on your finger to remind yourself, it may not impress her, but the fact that you discipline yourself to do it shows that you are dedicated to meeting her need and, therefore, it is the highest form of love.

In all of this, we are recognizing our spouse's need and responding to it. As her husband, how can I do any less? If she is willing to keep track of how many times we make love each month so that my need is met, then I must do my part to see that I am meeting her needs as well.

In his book *If Only He Knew*, author Gary Smalley[5] tells of a time when his wife shut down emotionally and didn't speak to him for two years. Rather than abandon her, he learned how to woo her again by making her know how important she was to him. In the book he shares how that worked.

It is a small and easy-to-read book, and I recommend it to men everywhere who want to learn how to meet the need of their wives in this regard. Women,

not a good idea to buy the book and lay it open on the night-
our husband will feel pressured to read it. Let him discover it for
let him go out and buy it and read it on his own volition. That
way he will appreciate it much more.

Men, if you love your wife, you'll do it. Reading the book, or other good
books about a woman's needs, is another way that you can say, "I love you." If
Christ gave Himself for the Church, and He is our example, then we can put
forth whatever effort is required to learn to meet our wife's needs.

The Issue of Respect

Second to sexual needs, the most oft-repeated complaint of men is this:
"She doesn't seem to respect or admire me." Well, just as we express to our
wives our need for sufficient sexual activity, we must also express to them whatever else we consider to be a need. If not, how can they know?

It might be helpful for you to try putting into writing your list of needs.
The process may help you clarify them more in your own mind and even to
better express them to your mate.

Once that is accomplished, you might want to list some action steps you
would consider appropriate for meeting the need. It's not as easy as it sounds,
and you may struggle with it, but it will pay off in the long run.

I say this from experience. On my desk, among other files, is one marked
PERSONAL. In that file is a dog-eared piece of paper that has been with me
for many years now. On that paper, Lorrie wrote her needs and the action steps
I would have to take so that (if I did them all consistently) she would be content in each area of need. I have kept that paper ever since.

Somewhere in her dressing area at home she has a similar piece of paper
containing a list of my needs and the action steps I considered necessary. Our
needs haven't changed in these many years, and we want to keep them ever
before us.

Every once in a while, Lorrie gets her sheet out and reviews it, and I do the
same. We talk about our needs four times a year, when we do our quarterly get-
aways. We take the lists with us, and then we discuss them. I ask her,
"Sweetheart, how am I doing at meeting your needs? Is there anything we need
to add to the list? Are there any of the action steps that no longer make sense

to you?" In this way, we keep each other's needs always uppermost in our minds.

If a man feels the need to be admired and respected, he might write down some action steps like the following to suggest to his spouse:

- Be proud of me in a group setting and let me hear you building me up.

- Find value in my advice and opinions.

- Compliment me when I speak or when I do some special project. (Typical men are just overgrown boys, and they need encouragement. "Come out here and see what you think of this," we say to our wives. And what they say means everything in the world to us.)

- Since we are called to be the spiritual leader in the marriage and the family (we didn't ask for it), then our wives should respect us in that role. We agree not to use the Bible to hit them over the head, but we need them to agree to honor what we say so that our children will also respect us.

- Allow me to pay and to take the lead when others are with us.

- We can take turns driving clear across the United States, but when we arrive at our destination, let me be behind the wheel. (I know that it's a stupid male ego thing, but it's real, so humor me.)

Your list may be different.

Please don't despise a need expressed by your spouse. It may sound foolish to you, but it's very real to them, so don't make fun of it or belittle them because of it.

You don't have to understand a need or even agree with it or like it. You only need to recognize it and meet it. That's your responsibility.

Men will probably never fully understand women and how they think, and women will probably never fully understand men and how they think. If you're married, just accept this fact and get on with life. If her needs seem stupid to you, your needs probably seem even more stupid to her.

Yes, I understand that in your thinking your needs are completely rational, but I also know that in her thinking, her needs are completely rational. Accept the difference of opinion, and stop fighting each other. You're on the same team.

The Issue of Spiritual Leadership in the Home

The second most common complaint that I hear from women is this: "I need him to be the spiritual leader." For some reason, that phrase makes a lot of men quake in their shoes. What all will she require of him? Does she expect him to pray forty hours a week? Is she expecting him to have a fresh Bible study prepared every evening for the entire family? What does being the spiritual leader really mean?

You women should prepare some proposed action steps to present to your very nervous husband. Your action list may include some points like these:

- Pray with me every day. (Lorrie needs me to do this, so even if I pray on my own, we join hands every morning and evening and pray together.)

- Lead our family in a devotional once a week.

- Let me know from time to time what you are hearing from God. (Men, women like to see us reading our Bible.)

- Take the lead in making sure that we all worship together in church each week. (This means I need to be sure everyone is up and getting ready so that we can be on time. Obviously, if I'm lying in bed late saying, "I'm not sure I want to go this morning," that will not do much to inspire my wife and children. If our wives have to coax us to get up and go to church, we are not the spiritual leaders of our family. Insist as Joshua did, *"But as for me and my household, we will serve the Lord"* Joshua 24:15, and then actively help your spouse and children with their spiritual pursuits and in the struggles that ensue as they face the world. Sit down with them individually and challenge their faith. Talk to them about it. Even though my children are older now, I still do it. That pleases Lorrie. It was one of the action steps she outlined for me many years ago.)

The Issue of a Neat and Orderly House

Another frequently voiced complaint of men is their need for a neat and orderly house. Personally, I am enough like a woman that if the house is messy, then I'm a mess too. If the fence is broken, then I'm broken. When we had carpet installed in our house, and it took the installers five days to do the job, I was discombobulated all five days.

Our house is my sanctuary. That's where I go to retreat, to find peace. The rest of the world is a hectic place for me, so I need the house to look right.

I try to participate in the neatness of the house, picking up after myself and not expecting Lorrie to do that for me. But when I walk into my castle, I expect to see it neat and clean, and then I feel safe there.

For another person, this might be only a wish, a desire. For me, it's a necessity. I can't make it without it.

We have a rule at our house: The last person out of the bed makes it. And we don't leave clothes lying all over the bedroom. Some people can't see the urgency of this. They say, "Why make it? You're going to sleep in it again tonight." I can only answer: "Humor me." Having the bed made and the clothes picked up is part of the order I need in my environment.

So what might the action steps look like?

• To have a cosmetically neat house

• To have clothes put away

• To have the bed made every day

Once I had told Lorrie what I needed and suggested some action steps to accomplish it, then she knew how to please me. I had taken the time and made the effort to educate her.

The Issue of Communication

Women need communication. This can be scary to a man. What might it require?

• You may need him to be a focused listener. (As a polyphasic person, one who can do two things at once and do them both well, I can watch television and talk to someone and know what's going on in both worlds. I have also developed my ability to listen because I get paid for listening. I can carry on a conversation and read a book at the same time and tell you what I have read and what the other person has said. But, when it comes to conversation with Lorrie, I realize that she needs my attention. She needs me to be looking directly at her.)

- You may need him to talk to you the last hour of every day. (As I said before, some experts recommend that married couples converse fifteen hours a week. When do you have time for all of that? You figure it out. Lorrie and I have chosen to spend the last hour of every day conversing with each other. That's very important to her.)

- You may need him to hear and understand you, rather than try to problem solve while you're still speaking. (Men are often guilty of just wanting to get the matter over with quickly and therefore rushing her through what she is trying to say or cutting her off entirely to make some point. What women often need is just a sympathetic ear and an encouraging word. "Oh, you poor Baby, I'm so sorry that happened," will go a long way to comfort and assure her of your love and caring. Lorrie and I have an agreement. I never offer a solution unless she asks me for one. Otherwise, my role is as listener, "understander," and comforter.)

- You may need him to speak your language. (Gary Chapman, in his book *The Five Love Languages*,[6] explains that women are emotional, and we must communicate with them from an emotional point of view. Unless they ask us for practical advice to resolve a problem, it should not be offered. Let her understand that you care what she is experiencing. Often that is all that is required.)

- You may need him to concentrate on one issue until it is resolved. (Don't flip from one issue to another on her. That may be a tactic that helps you get the upper hand, but you will lose in the long run.)

The Issue of Maintaining Attractiveness for a Spouse

Not everyone has this need, but many do—especially men. It may be a weight issue.

If you are dating someone who was previously married, you may have to look at their weight when they were married rather than their weight now as their "normal" weight. Many people, men and women alike, no longer seem to care about their appearance once they have landed a fish.

Single people are notorious for dieting, exercising, and losing weight. Before I married Lorrie, I was running four miles a day, and both of us were going to the gym. Now, I can't remember the last time I ran.

I say good morning to the exercise equipment in my basement, and that's about as far as I get. There's a treadmill, a stair-stepper, a cross-country skiing machine and more. I finally gave away the bicycle when we hadn't used it for so long. It all looks lovely, but I don't use it. The moral of the story is that what single people look like is too often temporary.

To some spouses, it doesn't matter what their mate looks like, but to others (many others) image is very important.

To some spouses, it doesn't matter what their mate looks like, but to others (many others) image is very important. If you are no longer attractive to them, then that can be a serious problem. Marriages have ended because of this neglect.

If your mate has certain expectations in this regard, then you need to know that, and you need to do whatever is necessary to live up to those expectations. Perhaps you need to establish between you exactly how much weight one or both could gain before something serious would have to be done to reduce or, at the very least, to stop gaining.

Some people have a medical problem that needs to be addressed. It may be an underactive thyroid, for example, or even something more serious. If a medical problem cannot be addressed, a spouse can usually handle that. But if your response to them is "I don't care," that's a very different story. Most men can't handle that.

Some of the women I work with complain to me in counseling sessions, "Before we were married, he promised to exercise and lose weight, but he hasn't done it. He just keeps getting bigger." If that was indeed a promise, then there is an even more serious problem, a betrayal of trust.

This is not to say that men should always expect their wives to look like a model. Most models are not the typical size and weight. Expectations should always be reasonable.

If this is important to you, some appropriate action steps might look like this:

- Stay stylish in your clothes, and don't become frumpy. (This doesn't mean that you have to spend a lot of money, just enough to look nice.)

- Stay current in hairstyle and makeup. (If you have hair that looks like it came out of the 1950s, you're in trouble.)

- Keep your weight under control. (You may have to come up with some agreed-upon signal to let each other know when the line has been crossed.)

- Dress so that I'm always proud of you. (You may not want to spend any money on clothes right now, but if he has a need in this area, you must do it to satisfy his need. If he needs you to look stylish for him, that doesn't take anything away from who you are. "Well," some might say, "can't you just love me the way I am?" Okay, then, are there no guidelines at all? No barriers that need to be avoided? Why not just gain three hundred pounds and then demand and expect that he love you anyway? Would that be reasonable? You don't have to agree with his need, but if he has it and it's real, you need to meet it, or you may regret it.)

The Issue of Non-Sexual Affection

Women need affection that does not necessarily lead to sex. Their action steps might include.

- Hold my hand when we walk together. (Let him know if this means in the mall, down the street, or where. Be specific. Teach him what you need.)

- Hug me more. (Hug you when? When you wake up? Before you go to sleep? When he comes home from work? When he goes to work? Be specific. Teach him what you need. Some men just disappear without saying a word, and this leaves their wife wondering. Lorrie and I have an agreement. When either of us goes to the store we approach the other, kiss them, and say, "I'm going out to the store for a minute, Darling. I'll see you later." That leaves a spouse in peace. Discuss it and know what the action steps are.)

- Hold me, and kiss me. (When? How often? Be specific. Teach him what you need. Don't leave him in the dark. And, there are different kinds of kissing. A peck on the cheek is very different from a passionate kiss. Tell him what you need.)

- Give me a back rub. (How often? How long? If he doesn't know how, he'd better learn quickly. And he cannot say, "That takes too much effort for me." If she has expressed a need in this area and has communicated certain action steps she requires, then it is his responsibility to fulfill her need.)

The Issue of Recreational Companionship

Many men need recreational companionship. One man with whom I counseled said he needed his wife to become involved with him in softball. He and a group of his friends had the habit of getting together on Friday evenings to have a barbecue and play softball. It was rather a community affair that meant a lot to him. She had to learn to like softball.

Many women positively hate football, but if he wants to go to a pro game, don't send him with someone else. Go with him yourself.

If it's camping, learn to enjoy it.

If it's walks in the outdoors, make the best of it.

In his book *Love Is a Decision* Gary Smalley[7] tells the story of a couple who attended one of his retreats. Because there had been a discussion of meeting your husband's needs (with the suggestion that you find a hobby you can enjoy together), the lady decided to go deer hunting with her husband the next time he went. For her birthday that year, he bought her a hunting rifle, and she went to a rifle range and took lessons until she felt confident with her shooting ability.

Deer hunting season finally arrived, and they set out for his favorite spot. He made sure she was dressed and armed properly, and then he sent her off one way into the woods (the best place to see a deer), and he went off another way (with not nearly as good prospects). Before long, he heard shots coming from her direction, and he headed over there.

As he approached the spot he knew her to be, he heard a man's voice: "All right! All right! I said, 'All right!' All right, lady, you can have your deer ... just let me take my saddle off of him first." Apparently, she had accidentally shot someone's horse. Anyway, the lady was trying to please her husband, so we have to give her an "A" for effort.

You may insist, "I absolutely don't do hunting," but if your husband needs you to, then you do now.

He may say to you, "Learn to play golf with me," and golf may be the last thing you want to learn to play. But do it for his sake. You'll be glad you did.

What To Do with Your Lists

After you have given much thought and prayer to your list, write it out, along with the action steps you want your spouse to perform. Then exchange those lists with each other.

This is an important point in the marriage. Suddenly, you know, not only what your mate's specific needs are, but also the action steps necessary to meet those needs. In this way, your spouse has taught you what is important to them.

Fulfilling your spouse's needs may not be easy, and it may require discipline on your part, but you have no alternative. This is your responsibility.

A very important note to this entire subject of needs is that neither spouse can demand that their needs be met. Never! It doesn't work that way. A demanding person is an arrogant person, a hard and calloused person, an egotistical and narcissistic person, and such a person is difficult for anyone to live and work with. Rather than demand that your spouse meet your needs, you must love them in such a way that they will *want* to meet your needs. It must be a mutual desire, or it will not work.

Sometimes the desire to meet needs will not be mutual, and the result will be that needs will not be met. And what should you do then?

The normal reaction of most of us is: "Okay, if you're not going to meet my needs, then I'm certainly not going out of my way to meet *yours*." Although this may be a normal response, it won't help anything, and will almost certainly make matters worse.

Try this instead. Continue to meet your spouse's needs, following Christ's teaching by doing unto them as you would have them do unto you. At the same time, lovingly make it known that there are some unresolved issues in how your needs are being met.

"We need to talk when things cool down," is one way to approach it. "There are some things here that I don't feel very good about, and I want us to be the best couple we can be." Don't push it; just let it be known.

Whatever you do, don't get discouraged. If you do, and you stop meeting your spouse's needs too, the two of you may very quickly get sucked into the sinkhole that swallows up so many marriages these days.

Make a commitment to the needs of your spouse.

Make a commitment to the needs of your spouse. This will require that you put forth whatever effort is necessary to learn to love them in the way they need you to love them and that you show the necessary discipline to stick with it until you get it right. And you can do it.

Many people have been married for years, and yet they have never come to understand their spouse's needs and how to respond to them. Some have never understood that it is their responsibility to meet those needs, and others simply have not cared. Whatever the case, it is never too late to start. Even a couple in deep conflict can turn things around.

First, forgive each other for the failures of the past, and then start meeting each other's needs, and you will be amazed at what happens. Your relationship will suddenly take on new life, and before long what had withered and dried will begin to bloom again.

You can have a wonderful relationship with the person to whom you are married—if you will allow them to become your teacher. Don't be offended and reject them if, in the process, they tell you that you're not yet doing well enough in a certain area. Only they know what they need, so take their word for it, and keep working at it until you get it right.

Finally, pray and talk to God about these issues. Marriage was His idea, and He knows how to make it what it was intended to be. Ask Him to start with your heart first. You get your part right, and many times everything else will then fall into place.

In any case, you can't change anyone but yourself, so start there. When you are what God wants you to be, your spouse will respond to you and your needs.

The Role of Sex in a Godly Marriage

(Or What Hath God Wrought?)

Eat, O friends, and drink; drink your fill, O lovers. Song of Solomon 5:1

Many consider the topic of sex to be much too steamy for a Christian book, but God invented sex, and He did it for our enjoyment. As I stated earlier, it is one of the most important glues that hold the marriage together.

Because this is such a heavy topic to some, I always begin my teachings on sexual matters by telling a good clean joke:

A man was speaking to group of several hundred people on this subject, and he decided to take an informal poll. "How many of you make love three hundred times a year?" he asked. Interestingly, some people raised their hands. He counted the number and jotted it down.

"How many of you make love two hundred and fifty times a year?" he continued, followed by, "How many of you make love two hundred times a year? … One hundred and fifty? … One hundred?"

61

He continued to work his way down until he was now feeling sorry for those who responded, but out of politeness, he forged ahead. "How many of you make love fifty times a year?" "… twenty-five times…?" "…ten times…?" "… five times a year …?"

It seemed that he had come to the limits of his poll, but he decided to add one more question, "How many of you make love one time a year?" To his amazement, a man at the back of the room waved his arm exuberantly, indicating that he was among this group.

"Sir, did you understand the question?" he asked.

"Oh, yes!" The man responded. "You asked how many people make love once a year. That's me."

Perplexed, the speaker dared to ask another question: "If it's true that you make love only once a year, sir, what, may I ask, are you so excited about?"

With this the man at the back stood and, waving his arms even more excitedly, declared, "Today's the day!"

"Why do we even need to mention sex in a Christian book about marriage?" some might ask. Let me quote from a letter I received, and you will understand better where I'm coming from:

A Poignant Letter

Dear Larry and Lorrie:

I've enjoyed your classes greatly, and I'm only sorry they're ending. I wanted to tell you something about my particular case. When my wife and I married sixteen years ago now, we were a great combination. Everything I loved she loved. We wanted to go the same places and do the same things. We enjoyed the same restaurants and the same music, and we both loved camping and picnics—to name just a few things. These were all the reasons we fell in love and married.

But what happened? Now we seem to be complete opposites. I still enjoy those same things, but she enjoys none of them. She tells me that was all in the past and that I need to grow up. We seem to have nothing in common anymore.

It gets worse: I haven't had sex with her in six years and haven't seen her naked in seven (she always locks the bathroom door when she's in there). When I attempt to have sex with her (something I haven't tried in many months now), she tells me that it's disgusting and shameful and that I should go pray and ask for God's forgiveness. She has even suggested that if I simply must have sex, I should go find a prostitute to do it with. Do other Christians have these problems? Please help us!

It is the impassioned plea of a man who has been married for a very long time, but who realizes that part of his marriage is dead. Unfortunately, I never knew who wrote the letter (it was unsigned) and, therefore, I was not able to help the man personally. But because of his letter and others like it, I have made it a point through the years to attempt to have some positive input into the lives of all those whom I have counseled.

What I can say in general about sex is that God intended for it to be great among marriage partners, but that Satan has done his best to demean and weaken the experience. Because we live in a world obsessed with sex, many Christians have decided that sex is dirty and sinful.

Since Lorrie and I have been married, we have been totally faithful to each other, but because I was married before, and Lorrie had been sexually promiscuous before we were married, we understand many of the issues that arise around this subject. Lorrie's pain journey took many years to heal on the path of restoration to sexual wholeness.

I went into my first marriage as a virgin, without any preconceptions of what sex in the marriage should be like. Lorrie, unfortunately, carried a lot of baggage into our relationship, and it has taken her years to shed it. This has caused us both pain.

Sex is not dirty. It is a beautiful gift from God to His children and, as such, it is pure and holy. It is Satan who has tainted sex. He took what God intended for good, twisted it into something ugly and sleazy, and now uses it for his own purposes. But we must not allow this fact to rob us of what God intended for us in marriage. Sexual intimacy is an integral part of the marital relationship, a part that needs to be conducted in God's order, and a part that we need to get right. Much is at stake.

"Should the church be addressing issues of sex?" Absolutely! The blasé attitude of many in the church on this matter is sad because several of the problems the church is facing revolve around sex: teenage pregnancy, abortion, adultery, moral failure among church leadership, and homosexuality. These are issues nearly every church has to deal with on a regular basis, so why are we so hush-hush about sex as God intended it? By insinuating that sex should not be mentioned in the church, we are falling into the very trap of the enemy.

"Should the church be addressing issues of sex?" Absolutely!

God's idea for sex was holy, and it is an act that He Himself instituted. He made man, and He made woman, and He made man for woman and woman for man. And He did all of this at the very beginning:

So God created man in his own image, in the image of God he created him; male and female he created them. God blessed them and said to them, "Be fruitful and increase in number; fill the earth and subdue it...."
Genesis 1:27-28

The union of man and woman was part of the foundation of our relationship with God and with one another. God is so awesome that He could have done it any way He wanted to, but He wanted to do it this way, and He did.

If anyone doubts that sex is of God and that He instituted it for a holy purpose, they should read the book of the Bible known as the Song of Songs or the Song of Solomon. The entire book is dedicated to the art and beauty of lovemaking. If that were somehow dirty, God would never have permitted that particular book to become part of the sacred Scriptures. In fact, God decided that the one book He would give to us for eternity, a book that would stay relevant to all generations, should devote one of its sixty-six parts to the subject of sex.

The Song of Songs is not the only book of the Bible that mentions sex. This subject is discussed very frankly throughout the Bible—from Genesis to

Revelation, and all Christians need to read and study what the Bible says about sex and then begin teaching their children God's attitude about this all-important matter.

The problem is that there are many confusing and conflicting messages about sex swirling around us. Sex is being taught to our children, not from the purity of the Word of God, but through the unhealthy attitudes of the popular media. Like the woman in the letter I just quoted from, many Christians have come to the mistaken conclusion that because sex is so abused by the world, it is bad in itself and should be shunned and avoided. Nothing could be more deadly to a marriage.

Why is the divorce rate among Christians almost identical to the divorce rate for other Americans? Something is wrong, terribly wrong. Christian men and women are not having their needs met in their existing relationship, and this must change.

A Spiritual Union

God's vision for human sexuality was clearly one that went far beyond a physical mating. His intent was a spiritual union, something that many seem unable or unwilling to understand or appreciate. Too many see sex as little more than another bodily function, but believe me, it is far more than that.

It is time for us to learn, to practice, and to teach all that God has to say in His Word about sex within marriage, but alas, many Christians seem totally uninformed. "What is right and what is wrong in sexual behavior? What should we do and what should we not do?" The fact that these and similar questions are being asked by churchgoing people shows that there is much confusion still on this subject.

Sadly, what most of us know about sex we learned as children from playmates or from the wrong kinds of friends. When we grew up, we therefore had ideas, attitudes, and beliefs about sex that had been preformed by this limited, and often corrupted, input.

Others learned nothing about sex as children, and therefore they grew up in total ignorance about the subject. Some grew up learning from the example of parents and other relatives and neighbors. Often these were bad examples, and they bred bad attitudes in those who observed them on a regular basis.

Sadly, many of us have dragged this type of bad attitude into our marriages.

A client reported watching his parents kiss when he was a child, but what he remembers most is that his dad would always turn away, leaving him with the impression that kissing was somehow bad. Later in life, his parents were much more open about their relationship, but as he grew up, this negative image is what he carried away.

Some of our church fathers left us with unhealthy attitudes about sex. Augustine was sorely tempted in this area and has been widely quoted as saying that sex between married adults was okay, but that desire and passion were sin. Martin Luther, who remained a bachelor for many years, voiced similar sentiments. This attitude has been taught by many church leaders, and in general, we can say that a rather unhealthy attitude has been projected from the great majority of our pulpits.

As we have noted, attitudes toward sex in the twenty-first century are being taught by the popular media: television, movies, magazines and books, many of which are inspired by a spirit very foreign to Christian values. I cringe every time I go through the checkout line in the grocery store these days. The tabloids herald the latest purported scandals, and the popular magazines shout out their headlines: "Six Different Ways to Achieve an Orgasm," "Sexual Orgies Are Good for Team Building," "Ten Ways to Make Hot Sex."

It is very difficult to find a popular television program in which a healthy attitude of lovemaking is portrayed between two married people. Everything on the small screen these days seems to be premarital sex, adultery, or homosexuality.

If God said things about sex in the Bible, He must have done that for a reason. He must have known that we would need such teaching. He must have intended His Word as a manual for us, a sort of blueprint for marital relationships. Here are a few general things I can say about God's gift of sex.

The Gift of Sex

God has given us the gift of sex that we might create life:

God blessed them and said to them, "Be fruitful and increase in number; fill the earth and subdue it...." Genesis 1:28

God had a plan that He wanted to fulfill, and it involved His people having healthy sex.

God gives us the gift of sex for intimate oneness. He said:

For this reason a man will leave his father and mother and be united to his wife, and they will become one flesh. Genesis 2:24

God gives us the gift of sex for our pleasure. Although it is a holy act, it was also intended to be fun. Holiness and fun are not inconsistent, as some have imagined. God said:

Drink from your own cistern, running water from your own well. Should your springs overflow in the streets, your streams of water in the public squares? Let them be yours alone, never to be shared with strangers. May your fountain be blessed, and may you rejoice in the wife of your youth. A loving doe, a graceful deer—may her breasts satisfy you always, may you be ever captivated by her love. Proverbs 5:15-19

This is the pleasure that God intended for marriage.

God gives us the gift of sex as a defense against temptation. He said:

Do not deprive each other except by mutual consent and for a time, so that you may devote yourselves to prayer. Then come together again, so that Satan will not tempt you because of your lack of self-control. 1 Corinthians 7:5

I have counseled many men who said that their sexual appetite was the number one need in their relationship, and it is apparent that this often leads good Christian men into temptation. When they have not had sex for an extended period, suddenly they begin to look at women they would not have looked at otherwise. I encourage them to tell their wives when this happens. Wives need to know that their lack of affection can lead to destruction for their husbands.

God gives us the gift of sex for comfort. After the loss of their first child, *"David comforted his wife Bathsheba"*:

Then David comforted his wife Bathsheba, and he went to her and lay with her.... 2 Samuel 12:24

On many occasions, when I have come home after a very hard day, Lorrie has seemed to realize that what I needed from her was that she get out our bottle of massage oil and start rubbing my shoulders as a prelude to lovemaking. Later, as I drifted off contentedly to sleep, she must have felt fulfilled in having comforted me in this God-given way.

Women, your husbands are out there fighting the world all day long. When they come home, they need a very different type of atmosphere, a loving one, and a comforting one. And sex can be part of that.

Through our lovemaking, we can create life, we can experience the one-flesh intimacy, we can enjoy deep pleasure, and we can even comfort each other in times of sorrow or trouble. Will you choose what the world says about sex? Or will you choose to go God's way?

The Consequences of Sexual Sin

I would be remiss if I failed to address in this book the consequences of sexual sin. Lorrie suffered terribly in this regard, and her past haunted her for far too many years of our marriage.

But she is not alone. Brian Keith Williams, a pastor in Columbus, Ohio, stated in his video series "Sanctified Sexuality" that 75 percent of the church is or has been bound by sexual sin. Imagine it! Seventy-five percent! That's a huge number of people.

The consequences of premarital sex can include separation from God and from fellowship with Him. We all know that His Word is very specific when it tells us what we can do and what we cannot do, and it declares that the consequence of sin is death (see Romans 6:23). When we disobey God, therefore, we choose death and are separated from Him.

Although the death that results from sin is not usually a physical one, in some cases, it can be. Spiritual death is always the result.

God's laws are not vague in any way. He has said, for instance:

You shall not commit adultery....   Exodus 20:14

Flee from sexual immorality.... 1 Corinthians 6:18

When we fail to obey these commands, we make the choice to enter into sin, and this creates a separation between us and God.

God is our loving heavenly Father, and out of love He will always discipline us. Then we must live with the consequences of our sin—whatever they happen to be.

One consequence of sexual sin has come to be called "spiritual fragmentation." During sex, there is a mystical union between the two participants. Each leaves a small part of themselves with the other and takes away a small part of the other with them. If they go on to have sex with other people, the effects of this multiply, and sometimes we can have a large crowd with us in the bedroom.

Paul wrote:

Do you not know that your bodies are members of Christ himself? Shall I then take the members of Christ and unite them with a prostitute? Never! Do you not know that he who unites himself with a prostitute is one with her in body? For it is said, "The two will become one flesh." 1 Corinthians 6:15-16

When a person is involved in premarital sex, or sexual sin of any sort, they join themselves with another person, and then another and another. This happens through sexual intercourse, or it can even happen through intimate touching or any sort of physical stimulation. Through that act, they have joined themselves with that other person, and a soul tie is formed.

If this has happened to you, you might experience any or all of the following symptoms:

- You have a heightened awareness of another person's needs, feelings, or activities, and this person is not your spouse.

- You feel as if you are constantly searching for a lost lover.

- You have the inability to feel fully joined and committed to your own spouse.

- You fantasize about other persons of the opposite sex while making love with your spouse.

- You sometimes feel incomplete because you have given yourself to another through intercourse or intimate touching.

- You frequently feel that sex is overrated and you could get by without it.

- You want people to quit talking about sex.

- You have some remaining mental or emotional bond to another person.

If any of these sound like you, you need some healing in your life. If you have been fragmented through sexual intercourse, sexual violation, or other forms of lovemaking with a person outside the bonds of marriage, God can restore you.

Let Him work to renew your love life just as He does to change every other aspect of your life.

Here is the process: First, repent of your wrongdoing, asking God to forgive you. If it is possible and practical, ask forgiveness from the other party. Then ask the Lord to break any spiritual links that exist between you and the other person and to restore you to sexual wholeness.

Place a special memento of your present commitment in a prominent place in your home as a reminder to you and to the enemy of your soul (for instance, we have a marriage covenant that we both signed hanging on the wall in our bedroom). When the enemy tries to come in and accuse you, let this serve as a reminder to him.

The Scriptures declare:

He who was seated on the throne said, "I am making everything new." Revelation 21:5

Let Him work to renew your love life just as He does to change every other aspect of your life. You may not return to virginity in the physical, but it can certainly happen in the spirit.

Spiritual and Sexual Wholeness

Spiritual and sexual wholeness are not unrelated. Before she yielded her life to God completely, Lorrie tried to separate the two. She would go out on Friday night and be sexually promiscuous, and then she would go to church on Sunday morning and try to worship God. But the two worlds cannot be separated; they are one. That's why God urges us not to become involved in premarital sex and not to practice lovemaking outside of marriage. He knew exactly what He was doing.

Our sex life must become more closely aligned with our spiritual life. Vonette Bright is quoted in *Intimate Issues*[8] as saying that it is as important to be filled with the Spirit in bed with your husband ministering to him as it is for you to be filled with the Spirit when you are teaching the Bible or ministering to others. Think about that! God designed the sexual union to be so holy that we can be just as spiritual in the bedroom as we can be when we are teaching a Bible class. That's His design, and it is only our own desires and the enemy's tricks that have caused us to deviate from it.

Sex can be just as holy as any other holy act. God said:

Eat, O friends, and drink; drink your fill, O lovers. Song of Solomon 5:1

God went right into the bedroom of the Shulamite woman when she and her lover were in the process of having sex with each other, and He's in your bedroom when you're making love too.

Did you ever make love to Christian music? You can do that, and it doesn't make God angry. It's not a sacrilege. It pleases Him. It's time to invite God into your bedroom—especially if you've had some premarital issues.

Sex is such an important part of your life with your spouse that if the enemy can creep up on you at some point and make you believe that making love to your spouse is boring and "not fun," he can do your marriage a lot of damage. Use the Word of God to "send him packing." Paul wrote:

We demolish arguments and every pretension that sets itself up against the knowledge of God, and we take captive every thought to make it obedient to Christ. 2 Corinthians 10:5

Learn what God has to say and then use His Word against any enemy that threatens you.

Begin praying more in the Spirit. You can do it together, and you can even do it before, during, or after you make love. There's nothing wrong with making God a partner in your most intimate affairs. In this way you can achieve sexual and spiritual wholeness.

The Law of Sexual Union

In his book entitled *Holy Sex,* [9] Terry Weir has stated that God has a law of sexual union. This is a natural law, as opposed to a moral law.

A moral law, like the Ten Commandments, can be broken, and there are usually consequences for breaking it. A natural law is even more serious. When you step off a cliff, for instance, the consequences are instantaneous and certain. They are guaranteed by the Law of Gravity, and it never fails. In the same way, there are always consequences for breaking God's law of sexual union. God said that we should run from sexual immorality because we are God's temple:

Don't you know that you yourselves are God's temple and that God's Spirit lives in you? If anyone destroys God's temple, God will destroy him; for God's temple is sacred, and you are that temple. 1 Corinthians 3:16-17

Flee from sexual immorality. All other sins a man commits are outside of his body, but he who sins sexually sins against his own body. Do you not know that your body is a temple of the Holy Spirit, who is in you, whom you have received from God? You are not your own; you were bought with a price. Therefore honor God with your body. 1 Corinthians 6:18-20

Making love with someone who is not your legal spouse, thus going outside of the marital bedroom, is a sin against your own body, and you *will* pay the consequences. Such sins also affect our soul, they affect our thoughts, and they affect our emotions. The writers of the New Testament show us how the mind and the body constantly fight each other for control. For instance, Paul wrote:

I have the desire to do what is good, but I cannot carry it out. For what I do is not the good I want to do; no, the evil I do not want to do—this I keep on doing. Now if I do what I do not want to do, it is no longer I who do it, but it is sin living in me that does it. Romans 7:18-20

The mind and the body are in constant conflict; the flesh wants to do one thing, and the spirit wants to do something else. When we yield ourselves to God, He takes up permanent residence in our bodies, and we become his home. Then, when you, as a believer, go out and make love with a person who is not your spouse, what are you actually doing? Think about it. God is in your body, and your body belongs to Him, and yet you are using it for sin. In this way, you are sinning against your own temple, and you are sinning against God, who has chosen to make your temple His abode. Learn to respect God's law of sexual union.

The Secret to True Sexual Fulfillment

The secret to true sexual fulfillment is not just in the physical act of lovemaking with another body. Holy sex is touching my spouse's spirit with my spirit *during* the act of lovemaking. Have you ever thought about that? Have you ever thought about going to that next level, far beyond the mere carnal act, and thus having an intimate, holy, spiritual relationship with your spouse just as the Shulamite woman did in the Song of Solomon? This is lovemaking as God intended it—the joining, not only of bodies, but also of souls and spirits.

Holy sex is touching my spouse's spirit with my spirit during the act of lovemaking.

John and Paula Sanford have stated that enjoying each other's body is thrilling, and feeling tender emotions of love is wonderful, but the embrace of your spirit by the spirit of your beloved is what provides true satisfaction in sexual union.[10] We want our spirits to join.

We can receive Jesus as our spiritual spouse, and He will love us through the body, soul, and spirit of the person we are married to. How wonderful!

Jesus lives in my wife, and when I make love to her, I'm making love to God. That is more than many people can fathom. Sex, in this proper context, can be just that wonderful.

Because the Lord dwells within my wife's body, my lovemaking with her becomes a holy act. With every caress and every gentle touch, I am expressing my love—not only to Lorrie, but also to the Holy God who created me, gave His life for me, gave us to each other, and now lives within each of us.

Men, can we fathom loving God with our spirit even as we make love to our wife and enjoy His presence in her loving us back? Can we leave the physical level of sex and go to another level, a spiritual level in sexual intimacy?

Understanding this truth will forever change the way you think about, look upon, and approach your spouse.

As men, we are often satisfied with the mere physical act of sex, but women always want more. They want us to show that we love them and that not everything we do is just to gain their sexual favors. And it is time that we, too, desire a deeper experience, a spiritual union.

That doesn't mean we won't have fun and that it won't be pleasurable, but our wives need to know that we regard our lovemaking as something very godly. Sex is a carnal act for Christians only if we fail to touch the spirit of our spouses with our own.

It has been said that a healthy sexual union accounts for 15 to 20 percent of marital satisfaction. If, on the other hand, your sex life (or lack of it) is a negative in your relationship, it will contribute anywhere from 55 to 70 percent of your marital dissatisfaction. If it's good, it lines up with everything else, but if it's bad, it's really bad, and it will negatively impact the marriage relationship.

In her book *Liberated Through Submission,*[11] Bunny Wilson made one of the most incredible statements I've ever heard. She said that the same spirit of rebellion that will cause a woman to be sexual outside of marriage will cause her to be unavailable sexually in marriage. With her blessing and approval, given when she and her husband Frank were speakers at one of our annual marriage retreats, I added a corresponding statement for men: The same spirit of rebellion that will cause a man to be sexual outside of marriage will cause him to be unable to be a spiritual leader inside of marriage.

When you defy God and step outside of marriage, you are saying, "I'm not going to follow Him. I'm not going to lead the two of us in the ways of righteousness. I'm not going to honor what the Word of God requires me to do as a spiritual leader."

Men, when the going gets tough in our marriages, we will be incapable of making any better decisions inside of marriage than we have been making outside of marriage. If you've been sexual outside of marriage, you'll have to repent and figure out what went wrong in order to return and be the spiritual leader God wants you to be within the marriage.

The Bible shows us that sex is a natural part of marriage, and the converse is also true: Sex is unnatural outside of marriage. Therefore, the rebellion that takes you away from God's plan and outside of marriage will also take you away from God's plan inside of marriage. Repent for being sexual outside of marriage and surrender to the will of God inside of marriage.

Men, I want to post a disclosure statement here for all to see. If you are being abusive, your wife will not want to make love with you (and she should not make love with you). We are required to love our wives as Christ loved the Church and gave Himself for it. The primary responsibility is on us to be the loving husband, and usually our wives will reciprocate in a wonderful way. Be abusive and everything changes.

Six Potential Problem Areas in the Sexual Arena

There are six potential problem areas in the sexual arena that we want to examine here:

1. Past Conditioning

The first potential problem area in the sexual arena is past conditioning. When you go into a marriage, you bring the baggage from your past life with you. Lorrie and I had this problem. There we were: I had a luggage cart; Lorrie had a luggage cart; and we were walking toward each other. It would have been so great if we hadn't had those baggage carts to deal with, but we did have them, and they affected how we would relate to each other sexually.

The sexual atmosphere in the childhood home is a primary determinant of sexual responsiveness in adulthood. We only know what we see growing up.

Personally, I saw nothing. My parents were loving to a certain extent only, and if I hadn't known better, I would have thought that, like Jesus, I was the product of an immaculate conception. The problem was that I had siblings, so my parents must have had sex at least a few times during their married life together.

The only sex instruction I ever received growing up came when I was a senior in high school. Because I had my arm around my eighteen-year-old girl-friend, I was told by my parents, "Son, if you don't stop that, you're going to have to get married." Later I realized that they meant that I was in danger of getting my girlfriend pregnant, but at the time I wasn't sure why my arm around her should lead automatically to marriage.

If touching and talking about sex are forbidden in the home, children decide that sex is dirty, ugly, and bad. They make their conclusions about sex by looking at us. An example might be: Dad comes home. He hugs and kisses Mom, and then he pats her on the rear. She turns and hugs him affectionately. What's the message they are relaying? That sex is good, and children will pick up on this every time.

What if the exact opposite happens? Dad comes home. He hugs and kisses Mom. But when he pats her on the rear, she responds, "Get your hands off of me" and slaps his hand away. What message does that send? If hugging and kissing are wrong and affectionate pats are worse, then sex must be horrendous. That's an unfortunate message to send to any child.

I'm not suggesting that we become exhibitionists in front of our children, only that we allow our children to see us in light sex banter, so they can know that it's okay for them someday. A man coming up behind his wife, hugging her and letting out a pleasant sound sends the right kind of message.

Ladies, you are teaching your children (especially your daughters) by how you respond to your husband's affections. If it seems to your daughter like some duty that you just need to get over with as quickly as possible, that is probably the attitude she will carry into her adult life.

Men, if the only time you warm to your wives is when you're on your way to the bedroom, you're saying to your children that the only time you have to be loving to your wife is when you want something from her. The result of that will be your sons learning inappropriate behavior that will bring them much unhappiness in the future.

What is the solution? Replace this prior conditioning, this baggage cart that you've brought into the marriage, with something more appropriate. Remove all the suitcases from your baggage cart, throw them aside, and then pick up the Word of God and its teaching in their place. The Scriptures declare:

If you hold to my teaching, you are really my disciples. Then you will know the truth, and the truth will set you free. John 8:31

Read the Song of Solomon. Read and reread the other portions of the Bible related to sexual intimacy. Then seek God's blessing upon this part of your life, just as you do upon every other aspect of it. When His blessing is upon your sex life, it will be good.

There will always be issues you must work through, but you can do that. Get the basics right, and other things will fall into place.

2. Differences in Desire Levels

The second potential problem area in the sexual arena (and it can be a huge one) is having differences in desire levels. But, so what if you have differences in desires? That's fairly normal with anything.

One of you likes carrots; and the other may not. Some are even allergic to carrots and can't eat them at all. That isn't a tragedy.

Lorrie likes chocolate ice cream, but I don't care for it. That's fairly normal and nothing to be concerned about—when each of you continues to treat the other with respect. For me to claim that because Lorrie doesn't like all the same things I do she's strange would be a bit ridiculous. In the sexual arena, however, this difference in desire can become a sharp bone of contention.

If I have a particular desire concerning the frequency of lovemaking and Lorrie has a different desire level, how can we go about resolving our conflict? The first thing we should do is share openly and honestly our differences. Usually it is the man who wants more frequent sex and the woman who could do with less. Men, make your desire clear to your mate.

There is a healthy limit. Men who think they need to make love many times every day probably have an addiction. They are taking something that is intended to be an expression of love between two people and making it into a codependency. They are trying to fill the hole in their heart and anesthetize their pain so that they can feel good again. That's not what sex was designed for.

I have a theory about the frequency of sex that I call my refrigerator theory. What if you had a refrigerator that had no handle on the door? You would not know how to open it when you wanted something inside. If it just opened occasionally on its own, that would leave you very frustrated. Would it be open when you were hungry? Would you be hungry when it opened?

Somehow I think that most of us would gorge ourselves every time it opened—whether we were hungry or not and even if we were sick at the moment. We would have to hang around the refrigerator constantly, just waiting and hoping for it to open. That would be very frustrating indeed.

Put a handle on the door, and all frustration ends. You know that you can open it when you want. If you're tired, you don't have to eat. If you're sick, you don't have to eat. You have the choice of eating when it suits you. Each of us needs to figure out how to make that same thing happen in the sexual arena. If we wait with uncertainty, hoping for lovemaking with our spouse, but not sure if and when it will happen again, our anxiety level will become elevated. But if we can determine a system for communication that allows us to openly discuss availability and frequency, the anxiety levels can be greatly reduced.

What is the *normal* frequency of sex in marriage? Actually, there is no normal. Normal is what two people decide works for them. There is, however, a benchmark, or average, that can be helpful. It is somewhere between two and three times a week. That doesn't mean that you and your spouse are bound by that rule. There is no rule.

If, on the other hand, you and your spouse have not made love in weeks, that's probably a sin. The Bible clearly commands us not to abstain in this way unless we are doing it for a spiritual reason (fasting and prayer, see 1 Corinthians 7:5). Even then, such a period of abstinence is only to be observed for a specific length of time. Not many of us are all that spiritual. Don't let weeks go by without making love to your spouse. And when a difference in desire levels is apparent between you, use the refrigerator system.

Many years ago a couple came to me for counseling, and they had a very great difference in desire levels. The husband's desire was not out of the ordinary, so I said to him, "What if you could go to that refrigerator anytime you wanted, and you could open it and take out what you wanted?"

His eyes lit up, and he said, "I would feel like a kid in a candy store."

I then turned to the wife. "What if you didn't feel like you had to have an orgasm every time you had sex with your husband, but could just be a willing and loving partner to meet his need? Would you be willing to make love to him more often?"

"That would be great," she said, and suddenly (and just that easily) the conflict that had most separated them was resolved.

Men are so predictable in this regard. Generally, they want sex, and they want it often. But women are much more complex creatures. For them to be interested in sex, it seems, there must exist the right configuration of stars and planets in the heavens. Of course, I'm exaggerating.

You're lying together in bed, and she hears a noise outside. "What was that?" she asks. The only sound he can hear is the pounding of his heart.

"Did you lock the door?" she asks. He doesn't care if there is a door at the moment; he is only interested in her.

It is said by those who have studied these matters that the average man has a sexual thought every fifteen minutes. That may be too conservative. It may be even more often. That's just how God made us, and it doesn't take much to stimulate us.

Men, understand that your wife may be tired, that she may have a lot on her mind, and that it may take a little longer for her—or a lot longer sometimes. Since the mind is the most important sex organ, be patient with her and work with her. And, if she doesn't want to achieve an orgasm every time, that's fine. If she finds pleasure in being your loving and willing partner, that's enough.

Now, be careful, ladies. Don't take too much for granted. You can't just say, "Okay, here's my body. I'm going on to sleep. Let me know when it's over." Unwilling or resentful participation is as bad as no participation at all.

Your cooperation in lovemaking also must not be only to repay a favor or to secure a favor. If you make love to your partner for any reason other than that you love him, it is not good enough. One woman I worked with had agreed to let her husband be in charge of their sex life in exchange for her being in charge of the money. That's not what God intended the sexual relationship to be.

So if one of you is more desirous of sexual intimacy than the other that's no big deal. Openly communicate your differences, and then work to resolve them.

3. A Failure of Communication

It is surprising how many couples never talk about sex. One man who attended one of our conferences told me that in thirty-one years of marriage, he and his wife had never once had a conversation about sex. They had several children, but how they did it I'm not sure. Apparently every once in a while, a sexual encounter just happened.

This may sound funny, but it is really sad. Why should we not discuss this very important subject? It is not shameful or degrading to talk about sex. If God can talk about it openly, then we can too.

Men, how can you not talk about sex? Your wife is not a mind reader. She can't know what you're thinking about. Is she supposed to know by your heavy breathing perhaps? You tell her when you're hungry. Why not tell her when you're hungry for her?

"Save me some time in your busy schedule this evening," you might say. "I want to make love with you." That's not too hard, is it?

One of the reasons men are sometimes afraid to approach their wives on this subject is that they're afraid to hear "NO."

It's better to state it this way than to ask her if she would like to make love with you. You might not like her answer. But just because she may not particularly want to make love right then, she may be willing to be a loving, caring participant in the lovemaking process for your sexual satisfaction.

One of the reasons men are sometimes afraid to approach their wives on this subject is that they're afraid to be hurt, afraid to hear "NO," afraid to be rejected. Stating it more as a positive desire on their part softens that possibility.

How and when do we decide to make love together? That's why God gave us mouths, vocal chords, and tongues. We have to talk it over, sharing our desires openly. Here are some issues you might want to discuss:

• **The Timing:** Some like to make love in the mornings, some in the afternoon, and some at night. Talk about it.

• **The Location:** Some like to make love in a variety of places, and others don't care about the place. Whatever you do, don't get stuck in a rut in the bedroom. You can make love in the car, on a deserted beach, in a forest, in a hot tub or bathtub, in the shower, on the floor in front of the fireplace—almost anywhere. Talk about it. (Yes, safety is a consideration in the location of your lovemaking. Make sure that no one might walk in on you at an inopportune moment.)

• **The Method:** How will you make love? There are a variety of ways to make love together, and it is good to have variety so that your lovemaking never grows stale. The danger is that your sex life will become mechanical. There is no right or wrong way, so experiment and find what works best for you. Talk about it.

• **What Pleases Your Mate:** The longer you are married, the better you will know your mate and how to please them. As you learn what they like, do it. And, although it can be very awkward, try to tell your mate what pleases you. Talk about it.

• **The Lighting:** Will you have the lights on or off? Often this decision is based on how well we like our bodies. Be sensitive to the desires of your mate. Talk about it.

• **The Attire:** You must decide how little or how much you will wear. Most experts in the field agree that the less you wear the better, but there are people who don't feel comfortable completely naked. They feel hot and sweaty, and it just doesn't work for them, at least to stay that way for a prolonged period. Honor your mate's preferences. Talk about it.

• **The Means of Stimulation:** Not all of us are stimulated by the same things. Learn what excites your mate. Each of us has fantasies. By this, I'm not referring to something born out of pornography or illicit sex, but out of personal desire. There may be something you have always wanted to do within the framework of a godly and loving relationship—make love in the rain, perhaps. Find what turns your spouse on and do it. Talk about it.

• **Non-Demand Pleasuring:** It is good to sometimes have a time of intimacy that does not end with sexual intercourse. Use this time to stroke your partner (anywhere except the genitals) to discover areas that are sensitive to your touch that you were not aware of before. This may wake up parts of the body that have not been used in a very long time. What feels good on your body? Let your mate discover it. Men especially tend to go immediately to the genital areas, but there are many other areas that can be stroked to bring your mate pleasure. Talk about it.

4. Situational Factors

There are a number of situational factors that can affect the quality of your sexual experience. For instance, if either of you feels rushed to perform sexually, nothing good will come of it. It's a little like someone standing over you demanding, "Go to sleep! Go to sleep! Go to sleep!" You can't do it under pressure. If situations pressure you to quickly come to an orgasm, you will more than likely fail. Good sex requires relaxation.

The first time we slept at Lorrie's parents' house after we were married, we made love in a bedroom she had slept in as a child. This made her very tense. Those who move in with their parents for a time will understand this.

81

If you have feelings of anger, guilt, frustration, or resentment, then you have some conflict resolution to do. Good sex is impossible between two people who are angry with each other. Apply the necessary forgiveness, and you will find your sex life improving.

Spectatoring is a term given to the act of pulling back to watch yourself perform sexually rather than being part of it. In good sex, we lose ourselves in the sexual relationship in total abandonment. Those who go into the marriage with a sexual past often struggle with the tendency to back away and become an observer. Deal with this tendency so that you can better enjoy your sexual encounters.

> *Good sex is impossible between two people who are angry with each other.*

Poor self-image, especially when it relates to body image, is another passion killer. For some reason, it took Lorrie a long time after we were married to fully realize that I liked how her body looked. For her part, she had all kinds of reasons why she didn't look good to me. For my part, she looked great to me then, and she still looks great to me now. If we make it to our seventies, she'll look great to me then, and if we make it to one hundred, she'll still look great to me.

The models who are used in the popular media are not typical in any sense of the word. Their type of figure makes up less than 1 percent of the population, they have received a lot of help, and even then, their photos have been doctored to make them look better. So don't judge your own body by something you see in a magazine. Don't be so hard on yourself. You spouse can't expect you to be more than you are.

5. Inadequate Information

Many married people don't have nearly enough information about physiology and human anatomy to know how the body works or is supposed to work. In his book *Sex Begins in the Kitchen* Kevin Leman[12] notes all of the pet names we sometimes have for the male organ. I have collected twenty-six of them myself. There are far fewer names commonly used for the female vagina—most of them vulgar. What message does this send? I'm afraid it sends the message that it's okay for men to play around sexually, but not for women.

Think about the host of popular humor surrounding male sexuality and the limited humor surrounding the female. This has caused many women to feel that their sexuality is somehow shameful, and they often come into a marriage relationship needing healing from this false perception.

Some women get married without knowing what an orgasm is, and consequently they don't know when they have one. If there is someone reading this book who still doesn't know, according to the *Merrium-Webster Dictionary* an orgasm is: "an explosive discharge of neuromuscular tensions at the height of sexual arousal that is usually accompanied by the ejaculation of semen in the male and by vaginal contractions in the female." It is a nerve response that makes you feel very good.

Some women are surprised when an orgasm suddenly overtakes them after many years of marriage. They were not expecting it and had no idea what they had been missing. It is also good to know that studies have shown that only about thirty percent of women can achieve orgasm during intercourse. They need further manual stimulation to achieve it.

Men, don't put undue pressure on your wife to have an orgasm. If she can't achieve it, that doesn't necessarily mean that you're a bad lover. Many women resort to faking orgasms, and they do it successfully for years. Although men can't fake it, women have the potential to do it well. Their intent is to let their man come away thinking that he has satisfied her, which can result in a deep violation of trust.

The book *Intended for Pleasure* by Dr. Ed Wheat[13] has many good teachings concerning helping a woman achieve orgasm. I recommend it highly. It is one of the best books on the physical anatomy written by a Christian.

6. The Rules for Acceptable Sexual Practices

Many Christian couples have no guidelines for deciding if some particular sexual practice is acceptable for them or not. We suggest the following criteria:

1. If the Bible does not forbid it, then it's okay. If it forbids it, forget it.

2. If no one is hurt physically, it's okay. If it might hurt you or your partner, forget it. It's not right.

3. If it offends either of you, don't do it. In the case that your offense is caused by past conditioning, seek to be healed of it. Otherwise, avoid the activity in question.

In our conferences and private counseling, we are often asked questions about specific sexual practices. These are legitimate questions, and we try to answer as honestly and openly as we can. Our answers are always based on these three criteria.

Plain Talk to Men

Men, women need to be romanced. Often their complaint is: "He just jumps on me long enough to satisfy himself, and then he goes right to sleep." Don't be guilty of this, men. Your wife needs your caring touch.

She also needs much more time to get ready for sex than you do. It takes, we are told, at least seventeen minutes of foreplay to arouse a woman sufficiently for sex. Be more patient, men.

Good sex begins with how you treat each other throughout the day. When you're already in bed and then you suddenly become amorous, your wife is turned off by that. Sex must not be the motive for caring behavior. That makes it seem to your spouse like you don't love them at all; you only want sex.

Many men have the macho idea that they know what pleases a woman. This is a false assumption. Don't assume anything. Become a student, and let your wife teach you what satisfies *her*.

Men, cleanliness is of vital importance to your wife. There is nothing romantic about the "manly" smell of sweat. If you expect your wife to make love to you more frequently, take a bath and smell good for her.

Don't be guilty of turning over and going to sleep the minute you achieve orgasm. The manly sound of snoring is not inspiring to any woman. And don't jump right up and run to the den to watch a ball game. Lovingly enjoy what has come to be called "the afterglow" of sex.

Plain Talk to Women

Women, men need to feel that they are sexually desirable to their wives. Sex is such a big part of who we are that if we think our wives don't want us and enjoy us, it is devastating.

Since men are visually stimulated, it is good for Christian women to put on some sexy lingerie or nothing at all for their husband's pleasure.

Women must not ever feel like they are the victims of their husband's desire. If you are not a loving participant in sex, he knows it, and he will be tempted to go elsewhere. This is important to your man.

There are several excellent books that are recommendable for Christian women who want to learn to please their man. *Intimate Issues* by Linda Dillow and Lorraine Pintus[14] from Colorado Springs, Colorado, *The Gift of Sex* by Clifford and Joyce Penner,[15] and *Holy Sex* by Terry Weir and Mark Carruth[16] are all good ones.

Now, enjoy each other, as God intended when He created you.

Communication and Conflict Resolution

(Or How to Have a Healthy Family Fight)

Put to death, therefore, whatever belongs to your earthly nature.... You used to walk in these ways, in the life you once lived. But now you must rid yourselves of all such things as these: anger, rage, malice, slander, and filthy language from your lips. Do not lie to each other, since you have taken off your old self with its practices. Colossians 3:5, 7-9

All of us have family fights, but the secret is to make them "healthy." The goal of healthy conflict is never to win, but always to resolve issues of conflict. If you insist on winning, then you will end up with one winner and one loser, and that's no good. Forget winning and seek to know how to resolve the current situation, how to manage your differences. That will result in two winners, and that's healthy.

Here are thirteen rules for how to have a healthy family fight, many of them from the wonderful book of the same name:[17]

1. Pick the Right Place and the Right Time to Have Your Fight

Pick the right place to fight, a place where you can work out conflict. Often, when couples get into conflict, one follows the other around talking to their back. It can be in the kitchen or around some other part of the inside of the house. You might find yourselves arguing outside or in the car. I suggest that you deliberately designate a place where you solve your conflicts. Find the place that's uniquely suitable for you.

...if you're not experiencing any type of conflict at all, something is probably wrong.

Seek a place where you can both be comfortable. There may be some heated discussion, and you will surely want privacy for that, but know that every marriage experiences conflict, and if you want to have a successful marriage, you must learn to manage it well.

In fact, if you're not experiencing any type of conflict at all, something is probably wrong. One party or the other must be swallowing natural responses, and this can result in even more conflict later on. It's healthy to raise issues that are important to each of you and then to work through them together.

If you have children, you will probably want them to be somewhere else when you have conflict resolution sessions. There's nothing wrong with allowing children to know that you have differences, but it is not wise to allow them to know the subject of your conflicts.

When you are ready to confront the matter, you might want to sit facing each other on two chairs in a room you choose, or you might want to be seated side by side on a couch. You may want to sit at the kitchen table and drink a cup of coffee or tea as you resolve your differences. Many couples like to talk in the car as they drive. This has definite advantages. (1) You have a captive audience, and you are a captive audience since neither of you can get away. Plus, (2) The ride seems to have a soothing effect.

Because I keep a counseling office at home, Lorrie and I have always been able to go into that office for our conflict resolution sessions. She never lets me sit in the counselor's chair during these sessions, however. I have to sit in the client's chair.

Once, when we seemed to be at a stalemate and could not resolve a particular conflict, Lorrie said to me, "Well, what would you say to some other couple if they were in here right now having this problem?" I put on my counselor's hat, thought for a moment, and then told her what I thought I would say. We tried it, and it worked.

There is one hard and fast rule about the place of conflict resolution: never attempt it in the bedroom—NEVER. You cannot afford the risk that your bedroom will ever become identified with conflict. Your bedroom must be a place for peace and calm and lovemaking. It must be a place where you draw closer together, not where you fight. If you do get into a fight in the bedroom, you should get up and go wherever it is that you do your conflict resolution and have any needed discussion there.

Just as carefully as you choose your place for conflict resolution, you must also choose the best time. That will never be in the middle of the night, and it must never be on your date night.

There are many other unacceptable times for conflict resolution. Once Lorrie and I were on our way to do a couples' retreat. We were driving on the Interstate about eight miles from the site of the retreat, when we suddenly got into an argument. It would have been different if we had been going to spend the night and then speak the next morning, but we would have to go to the platform and speak minutes after arriving.

We could not afford to arrive at that place fighting, so I reached over and took Lorrie's hand, and said to her, "We have an enemy who is setting us up. This isn't about us; this is about our enemy wanting to kill, steal, and destroy before we can even speak to God's people tonight." We prayed together, and the anger we had felt immediately lifted.

Notice that I didn't say that Lorrie was the enemy. We, the two of us together, have a common enemy who seeks to destroy our relationship.

If this common enemy attacks you on your date night or any other time you are trying to do something together to build friendship and trust, recognize him and rebuke him (not your spouse). Turn to prayer, saying, "We're not going to let this happen to us tonight."

Never use date nights as a time to resolve conflict. That's not the time to work out your differences. There will be a time and place for that, and it works much better if you have planned it in advance.

Never attempt conflict resolution when you are tired or particularly stressed out. One o'clock in the morning, just before you retire, is not the time to suddenly say, "By the way, I have a bone to pick with you."

One particular night Lorrie and I were in the hot tub, and she decided she wanted to talk about one of our children. But not only did I not want to talk about one of our children; I didn't want to talk about anything.

"I really don't want to talk about this tonight," I told her. "I've had a very difficult day, and I'm emotionally and physically exhausted. Can't we discuss this another time?"

"That's what you always say," she replied.

I realized that she had a valid point. If I was unwilling to talk about it at that moment, then I should at least tell her when I would be willing to talk about it. "Let's talk about it tomorrow evening," I suggested. And we did.

If you have put off talking about a certain issue until an appointed day and time, then you should be the one to bring the subject up. That's your responsibility. "You wanted to talk with me last night about something. Well, I'm ready now."

It is often the case that one spouse is quite articulate in any discussion, while the other is not. Setting a later time to discuss a matter gives both parties time to think over their position and to prepare the thoughts they want to share, so that they can be presented in a more persuasive way. It also gives both parties time to cool down.

When I get angry, I seem to have a silver tongue, and words just roll out of me. Lorrie, on the other hand, is just the opposite. When she's upset about something, she can't form her thoughts as well as when she is calm. I always prefer to fight right then and, of course, she doesn't. Long ago we agreed that either of us could ask for an hour break. When one hour has passed, if we're not ready to talk, we can ask for a second hour and a third. But that's it. When three hours have passed, we have to talk. We can't let the matter fester any longer. This rule has proved to be a good one, for it has saved us from many heated arguments.

Such a timeout is not a means of control. If you insist on controlling a situation, when it's not going your way, you will say, "I'm out of here; I'm not talking about this anymore." Your silence becomes a means of control. But asking for a break to better prepare yourself is something altogether different.

We have another rule that says that in these times of conflict resolution, neither of us can leave the property. One party leaving would give the other party the feeling of abandonment.

Another rule we have is that during that waiting period, we don't nag at each other. Each of us has the tendency to want to try to crash on through the other's boundaries and knock down their argument. We refuse to do this. Instead, we back off and give each other an hour to think.

Some years ago, we noticed that Lorrie sometimes suffered symptoms of PMS, and we learned to mark the calendar and to avoid any attempt at conflict resolution during those times. For a few months, we had seemed to always have some type of argument on those particular days, and this resolved it.

Ladies, if you experience mood swings during your periods, document it, and then don't make any major decisions during those days. If you are having a conflict, just back off and wait to see if it will pass with the season.

Once, when our daughter Carrie was only three or four, I walked by the table where she was sitting eating a hamburger Lorrie had told her to finish. I was hungry, so, in passing, I picked up the hamburger, took a bite of it, and passed on. Carrie finished the hamburger.

"Did Carrie finish her hamburger?" Lorrie asked me a little later.

"Yes," I answered.

"Except for the bite Dad took," Carrie added.

With that, Lorrie exploded. I had lied to her, and she was very upset about it.

This seemed so unlike Lorrie that I wondered what could have caused it, and then I suddenly knew. Rushing to find a calendar, I confirmed that it was *that* time of month. For the moment, all discussions were off. Nothing fruitful ever came of discussions during those particular days.

Choose the right place and the right time to have your fight.

2. Learn to Listen

The second rule for having a healthy family fight (and, perhaps, the most difficult one) is learn to listen. This is true with all of our communications.

God gave us two ears and one mouth so that we would listen more and speak less. Actively listening to one another during any discussion of conflict moves people closer to a resolution. If I'm listening to you, and you're listening to me, it's amazing how much progress we can make in a very short time.

Lorrie is a very good listener. The Scriptures admonish us all:

My dear brothers [this goes for the sisters too], *take note of this: Everyone should be quick to listen, slow to speak and slow to become angry, for man's anger does not bring about the righteous life that God desires.* James 1:19-20

This is a very critical scriptural teaching when it comes to communication in the marriage. Be quick to listen, be slow to speak and also slow to become angry.

Take inventory of your life by answering the following questions with "Usually," "Sometimes," or "Never":

- When my spouse is speaking, my mind wanders.

- When I disagree with my spouse, I shut them out of my listening. (You would be amazed at what I see sometimes in my counseling sessions. While one spouse is talking, the other is rolling their eyes, obviously disinterested and unimpressed by what is being said.)

- Even when I disagree with what my spouse is saying, I still remain attentive and listen.

- I interrupt my spouse when they are speaking. (When you do this, it shows disrespect. You don't feel that what they have to say is important, or you would rather not hear it. You finish their sentences for them because what you have to say is so much more important that you can't wait to say it.)

- I'm thinking about my answer while my spouse is speaking. (This is known as listening with your motor running, and you're probably not hearing a word that is being said. To you, your defense is the only important thing, so you're busy loading and cocking your guns.)

There are many barriers to effective listening. Choose the ones that fit you:

- **The Bored Listener**: This is someone who has heard it all before. They have their head cocked back, and their eyes are rolling wildly while the other person tries to speak.

- **The Selective Listener:** This person picks out bits and pieces of the conversation that interest them and rejects the rest. They hear only what they want to hear.

- **The Iron Trap Mind:** This person can quote back to you exactly what you said at some point. As much as you protest that it's not what you meant, they still insist, "Well, I don't care what you meant. That's what you said, and I'm holding you to it."

- **The Interrupter:** This person, rather than spend their time listening carefully to what is being said, spends it in forming their reply. And then they interrupt rudely to interject it.

- **The Insensitive Listener:** This person fails to catch the feeling, or the emotion, behind the words. When a son or daughter says, "You know, I don't think I'm going to do very well in college," this parent fails to realize that the child is frightened of the challenges ahead, or even afraid to leave home. "Nonsense!" they're told. "You're going to do just fine." And the underlying emotion of the child's words is ignored.

We must learn to use the language of the person with whom we are trying to communicate.

Adopt the Language of Your Mate

We must learn to use the language of the person with whom we are trying to communicate. For instance, it is quite common for two very different types of people to be drawn to each other and marry. One of them speaks from a cognitive point of view (that is from logic), and the other one speaks from an emotional, or feeling, point of view. Everything is interpreted to them according to how it feels. This makes for some strange and heated arguments.

Taking Lorrie and me as an example, if I said to her, "We're not making love often enough to suit me," she might immediately begin to cry and exclaim, "I will never be able to make love enough to suit you (or whatever else it happened to be)."

My first reaction to this usually would be not to bring the matter up again, for if I did, it would surely only complicate matters. Now, apart from my issue, I have a second issue to deal with: Lorrie is offended by the fact that I have any problem at all with our relationship.

Of course, this approach solves nothing. In time, I learned that what I had to say was this: "Lorrie, I need you to lay aside your feelings for a moment so that you can hear what I'm saying. Let's discuss this matter without turning it into something it's not. I understand that you're feeling pain, and I will be happy to address your issue when we have resolved the one we're talking about now."

In this case, because I brought up the issue and I am a cognitive type person, I got to choose the language we would use to settle the issue.

At other times, it might be reversed. Lorrie might bring up something that was bothering her in our relationship, and I could sense her pain and the emotion behind her words. In this case, it was not proper for me to ask her to put away her crying and discuss the matter rationally. She brought the issue up, so she got to select the language in which we discussed it. Eventually, my approach and hers would meet, and we would find a solution to our dilemma.

It was important for us to have set this ground rule before a crisis erupted. This was not something that we did decide, or could decide, during a conflict. If I had said to Lorrie in the middle of an argument, "Oh, quit your crying so that we can work this out," that surely would not have gone over well. It would only have intensified the argument, for she would then have been twice as angry and twice as hurt. The fact that we had set a ground rule beforehand that anything I brought up would be decided my way made it bearable and doable.

When we are discussing something with our spouse, and they get angry, then we become angry that they're angry, and there is no end to it. We suddenly lose the ability to communicate with each other.

Good Listening Habits Are Learned

There are prerequisites to being a good listener, and being a good listener is something you must decide to learn, not something you were born with. It is both a decision and a discipline.

We all hate to talk with someone who obviously cannot wait to get a word in edgewise. We know that the moment we pause for a breath they will jump in with their comments. Take a lesson from this, and when you are speaking with someone, pause a moment after they speak and catch a breath before you answer. Let it be apparent that the information they are giving you is being digested.

Good listening requires concentration and energy. It takes an effort on your part.

Good listening requires concentration and energy. It takes an effort on your part. It neither comes easily nor naturally.

Some have a professional listener look, but they only appear to be listening. The truth is that their thoughts are a mile away. Something that is said may spark a memory that leads them on a mental tangent far from the subject or the speaker.

We can actually sit and look at someone, nod at the appropriate times and grunt an occasional "yes," "uh-huh," "wow," or "how about that," and be somewhere else thinking about something entirely different. This often becomes apparent when the speaker asks a question related to what they are saying, and the listener has no idea what to answer because they don't have any idea what is being said.

Studies have shown that we only hear about 7 percent of what people are telling us. Those who are intent upon becoming a good listener must learn to focus. Here are some effective techniques for learning to be a good listener:

Be Quiet

The first important technique for those who would be good listeners is to be quiet. My, what a novel thought! Most of us need a little work in that area, don't we?

Silence in this context is okay. This is not a silence designed to punish. That type of silence is a form of control, and I have dealt with that in another section of the book. This kind of silence invites comment; it shows interest and gives opportunity for interchange. This kind of silence is not only acceptable; it is desirable. The Scriptures declare:

*There's a time for everything and a season for every activity under heaven:
…a time to be silent and a time to speak.* Ecclesiastes 3:1, 7

Take advantage of your opportunities to be silent and to learn from others.

Maintain Eye Contact

The next important technique for those who would be good listeners is to maintain eye contact with the person who is speaking. If you're trying to tell me something, and I'm looking all around or my eyes are following someone else who is passing, what does that say?

We knew one gentleman who would actually start walking away while you were talking to him. If you wanted to finish your thought, you had to follow him.

Try this exercise. Turn to your spouse, and with no talking and no giggling, look into each other's eyes for thirty seconds. I promise you that it will seem like the longest thirty seconds you have ever lived.

When we ask people to do this in a group setting, we can easily tell who the newlyweds are among us. Newly married people love to gaze into each other's eyes, but it seems that the longer we have been married, the harder this becomes.

Lorrie and I have a running joke. When we are traveling, we observe couples in public places and try to guess if they are married or not. Usually it's not very hard to do. If they are all wrapped up in each other's arms, we usually say, "Not married!" If they are walking apart from each other, we say, "Married!" Once, when we were in San Francisco, Lorrie was not feeling very well, so I walked across the Golden Gate Bridge and back by myself. Going across, I saw a couple all wrapped up in each other's arms gazing intently into each other's eyes. As I made the long walk back, they were still there, still holding each other, and still gazing into each other's eyes. When I told Lorrie about them, we both came to the conclusion that they definitely were not married. That's sad but often very true.

It has been said that the eyes are the windows to the soul, and we should not be hesitant to look into the eyes of the person with whom we are attempting to communicate.

If you have glasses and you don't wear them, you won't hear as well. That sounds strange, but a large part of our understanding comes from seeing the words formed on the person's lips, watching their gestures and facial expressions, and looking into their eyes.

Display Openness

Your nonverbal reaction to what people are saying to you is just as important as your verbal reaction. Smiles and good facial expressions speak volumes and invite conversation, while crossed arms and legs convey just the opposite message.

Listen Without Response

It isn't necessary to respond to everything that is being said to you—if it's obvious that you are listening.

Don't Switch Issues in Midstream

Switching issues in the middle of the conversation is one of the most commonly used forms of disrespect. As an example, I might say to Lorrie, "You know, it really doesn't feel good to me when you walk off and don't even seem to notice that I'm here," and she might answer, "Gee, are we feeling a little insecure today?" What she has done is switch the subject away from my hurt feelings. When someone is expressing a concern, don't be guilty of diverting attention to some other unrelated matter.

If Lorrie did this to me, I would say, "You may be right, and we can talk about that later, but that's not the subject right now. We're talking about you walking away and leaving me standing alone." It's possible to speak about fifteen different subjects and yet not resolve anything. Stick to the point at hand.

Another common way of flipping the subject is to turn it on the speaker. If I told Lorrie that I was hurt by the way she walked off and left me standing, and she said, "That's exactly what you do to me," and I answered, "No, I don't," and she answered, "Yes, you do," this could go on forever, and we obviously wouldn't get anywhere. Attend to the point at hand, and then you can go on to something else if necessary.

Provide Feedback

It's important that people know that they're being heard. Just nodding your head is helpful. You can say, "Uh-huh," or some other simple affirming response. Asking a question is even more affirming. For instance, when you ask, "What did you mean by that?" it shows that you are indeed listening. Your response says: "I'm hearing you, and I understand what you're saying." In this way, you are sorting things out as you go.

Learn to listen.

3. Control Your Tongue

The third rule for having a healthy family fight is control your tongue. I've heard it said that some people have tongues that could lick a spoon in the kitchen while they're still seated in the living room, and I think there may be some truth to that. James wrote to the Church:

If anyone considers himself religious and yet does not keep a tight rein on his tongue, he deceives himself and his religion is worthless. James 1:26

With the tongue we praise our Lord and Father, and with it we curse men, who have been made in God's likeness. Out of the same mouth come praise and cursing. My brothers, this should not be. James 3:9

Our tongues are really very powerful:

The tongue that brings healing is a tree of life, but a deceitful tongue crushes the spirit. Proverbs 15:4

Sometimes it is the heart that needs repair, because what we say with our tongues reflects what is to be found in our heart:

For out of the overflow of the heart the mouth speaks. Matthew 12:34

David sang:

Create in me a pure heart, O God, and renew a steadfast spirit within me. Psalm 51:10

I have hidden your word in my heart that I might not sin against you. Psalm 119:11

The Scriptures further declare:

Above all else, guard your heart, for it is the wellspring of life. Proverbs 4:23

The heart is deceitful above all things and beyond cure. Who can understand it? Jeremiah 17:9

God promised through the prophet Ezekiel:

I will remove from them their heart of stone and give them a heart of flesh. Ezekiel 11:19

I will give you a new heart and put a new spirit in you; I will remove from you your heart of stone and give you a heart of flesh. Ezekiel 36:26

Jesus said:

For out of the heart come evil thoughts, murder, adultery, sexual immorality, theft, false testimony, slander. These are what make a man unclean. Matthew 15:19-20

We clearly need to watch what we say, because it reflects what is in our heart. If we're not careful, when the hammer hits the thumb, what comes out will not be appropriate. You may say afterward, "I really didn't mean to say that," but there it is. Because your heart is wrong, when pressure comes and you suddenly find yourself in the vice of life, what's on the inside oozes out. And far too often it is not pretty.

The Five Levels of Communication

After we become willing to listen, we need to start concerning ourselves with how we respond. There are five levels of communication. Most people dabble around in the first three levels. They may jump to level four or five occasionally, but then they jump right back into the lower levels of communication. Every level is important, but the higher levels are essential to a successful marriage:

Level One

The first level of communication is small talk:

"Hey, Sweetheart, did you sleep well last night?"

"I slept great, thank you."

"Do you have a lot planned for today?"

"Quite a bit."

"Well, have a great day."

"You too."

Small talk is not bad in itself, and it is a necessary beginning, but if you never go beyond that level of communication with your spouse, you will be very disappointed in your relationship.

Some people seem to be so caught up in the hectic pace of modern life that all they have time for is small talk. But small talk is mere politeness. There is nothing intimate about it.

"Hi, Honey. I'm home."

"Did you have a nice day?"

"Yes. How'd the kids do today?"

"They did fine."

"Great."

"Well, good night. Sleep well."

"Thank you. You too."

Are we so consumed by the cares of the day that there's nothing left?

In this type of communication, we don't have to think, and we also don't have to be a very good listener. You're not giving anything of yourself, and your spouse is not giving anything of themselves to you.

Level Two

The second level of communication involves giving out facts with no personal commentary. If, for instance, Lorrie were to say to me, "Sweetheart, did you hear that the Broncos beat San Diego on Sunday?" She hasn't said if she was sad or happy about this turn of events, only that she heard it happened. She might as well be talking to a Raider's fan. She is not brave enough to tell me what she thinks.

100

It is surprising how many of us wait to express an opinion until we have heard what others think. That way, we will not risk being the first because our opinion might be rejected.

Level Three

In the third level of communication, we begin to express ideas and opinions. For instance, Lorrie noted the fact that the President had recently signed an order to build an American Embassy in Jerusalem, and she went on to say that she found this to be very exciting. We love Israel and have been there many times, and she felt it was about time we had representation in the Holy City.

By making this statement, Lorrie was taking the risk that not everyone would agree with her point of view, but at least she was willing to express herself. Expressing yourself in this way also gives others the opportunity to express an opposing viewpoint. Although many people avoid this type of conversation and stay with what is safe, most of us do eventually go this deep. It is to the next two levels that we are often afraid to go. In these levels, conversation sometimes gets really tough.

Level Four

The fourth level of communication involves feelings and emotions. This is where I take a knife, cut myself right down the middle, and begin to show Lorrie what is inside of me.

Some people do this much too soon in a relationship. As single people having a first few dates, they begin pouring out all sorts of personal information, almost as if they were vomiting all over their date. Suddenly, before the person is sure they want to know it, they become aware of facts and feelings that should remain sealed to most outsiders. These are the things we normally divulge only to those we love. Giving them away too early has a way of turning people off. Save it for more intimate moments.

On the other hand, many want to remain in the lower levels of communication long after they are married. The prospect of exposing themselves further terrifies them, and they shrink back from it, feeling much too vulnerable. Unless we are willing, however, to go deeper, we will miss out on the depths of personal communication.

Lorrie might say to me, "You know, when we were having dinner tonight, it was so much fun being with you, but my feelings were hurt because you kept answering the telephone in the middle of our conversation."

It is easy to see the risk she has taken with this communication. But she took the risk, and now the ball is in my court. I have two options for my response: I can either hurt her more by being insensitive to her feelings, or I can answer in a loving and sensitive way. The way I answer is important because it will determine whether or not she will be able to trust me with her feelings in the future.

Will Lorrie be afraid that I will hammer her every time she feels something? If I can handle this right, it just might lead us to the fifth and highest level of communication.

Level Five

The fifth level of communication is one we should all strive for and not be afraid of. At this level, we can relate both ways with some deep insights and caring. I might say to Lorrie, for example, that I can sense a lot of pain in what she has just told me and ask her to explain to me better what exactly I did that offended her.

In response, she might say, "When you kept answering the telephone and were willing to take time out of our dinner together to talk to anyone and everyone else, it made me feel that maybe our special time together was not as special as I imagined it was going to be. I was deeply hurt by that. After I thought about it for a while, I realized that it touched on my need to always feel special in your life."

Again, I would have some choices to make. I could respond to her with something like, "I'm really sorry I hurt you, but that was certainly not my intention." If I did that, I would learn from it, and we would have arrived at a new level of communication, one in which we were both pouring ourselves into the other and also not hurting each other in the process.

This is a dangerous point, because we are as vulnerable at this point as we will ever be. If we can respect each other's feelings, it will be worth it. Our intimacy will deepen.

What happens to most of us is that we get to level four, our partner opens up to us, and then we slam them. Afraid to stay at level four any longer, we retreat to the safety of level three and stay there. We may express ideas and opinions and facts, but we shun the temptation to go any further, for fear of being hurt.

This is sad because healing and intimacy take place at levels four and five, and if we're unwilling to go there, we will never have the relationship God intended us to have.

Communication Blockers

There are some communication blockers we should all work to avoid:

Explosive Words

One serious communication blocker is our use of explosive words. For instance, someone might say, "Good morning, Chubby! How's the diet going?" When those words are spoken, it is usually because the speaker knows just what buttons to push and how to push them to get a desired reaction. And such words almost always have the desired effect.

"Hey, Sweetie, those love handles are getting bigger every day."

One day I held up a photo of a body builder and said to Lorrie and Carrie (whom we call Sissy), "This is my body, but it's just waiting to pop out."

Sissy was quick to respond, "Why is it that only the stomach seems to be popping out?"

Someone might ask, "How long are you going to postpone cleaning your closet this year?" There always seems to be a barb on the end of our words, and we all do this to some extent. It is not Christ-like, however, and we often hurt people in the process.

What are the explosive words you use? You can know them by what you say as soon as you get in a fight. Sadly, our tendency is to go for the vulnerabilities of our "opponent." In this way, nothing is ever resolved. Rather than help each other, we do more harm to each other, and we postpone or forfeit entirely any hope of healing and/or deepening of the relationship.

The Silent Treatment

Another serious communication blocker is silence—pouting, sulking or the silent treatment. Please don't adopt this harmful habit. I speak from experience.

Very early in life I learned that if I had something to say, one of the ways I could be heard was to sulk or pout until someone noticed and asked me what was wrong.

"What's wrong with you?"

"Nothing."

"Oh, come on. Tell me. What's wrong?"

"Nothing."

But they could see that it was not true, and they kept it up until they drug the truth out of me. After a while, I didn't know any other way to communicate my problems.

As a teenager, I would sit quietly at the table until my father noticed. "What's wrong, Larry?" he would ask.

"Oh, nothing," I would say without much conviction.

"What's wrong, son?' he would insist.

"Nothing," I would answer in the same lifeless way.

Eventually he would take me out to the garage, and we would sit down and talk. Through an elaborate ritual we developed over time, he would eventually drag the truth out of me. Over time, this behavior became deeply ingrained in me.

I married what I thought was the perfect person in my first marriage, and when I started looking melancholy one day, she asked me, "What's wrong?"

"Nothing," I replied, as I had conditioned myself over time.

"Oh, come on," she coaxed, "what's wrong?"

"Nothing," I answered.

She, too, kept after me until she was able to drag the truth out of me.

This all changed when I met Lorrie. One day she noticed that I wasn't as happy as normal, and she asked, "What's wrong?"

I put on my melancholy face and replied without conviction, "Nothing."

"Oh, good," she said. "I thought for a minute there that something was wrong. Well, I'll see you later." And she was gone.

As Lorrie walked off, I was left feeling very frustrated. She didn't know how to play my game, as my father and my first wife had. In time, I learned that

Lorrie would give me about fifteen seconds to say what was bothering me, and if I didn't speak out in that time, she was on to something else. I also learned that this is the healthy way to get out our frustrations. Open up quickly and make yourself vulnerable to your mate. Get your feelings out in the open quickly and deal with them. Don't play games with something so important.

Those of us who learn to dance often learn wrong steps or moves. The partner we learned with may have been able to cope with those moves. They may even have been guilty of teaching them to us. But when we try to dance with others, it doesn't work, and something has to give. Either you have to change, or your dance partner has to change.

Lorrie had her way of dancing, and if I wanted to dance with her in this regard, I had to change. I decided that her way was best, so I was the one who had to make the necessary adjustment.

If you are silent, that might be conveying the message "I don't care," and an I-Don't-Care attitude in a spouse is very frustrating.

There may be other reasons for silence. Sometimes when someone asks us, "Why won't you talk to me? Why won't you tell me what's the matter?" the answer might be that we have learned that if we say something it will just be shoved back down our throat, so it's better for us not to say anything at all.

If there's something that I'm doing that makes it difficult for my spouse to share things with me, what can I do to create a safe place for communication in our home? This is the subject of the book *Safe People* by Henry Cloud and John Townsend.[18] In it, they define what they mean by a "safe" person, they give a means of taking inventory of yourself to see whether you are a safe or an unsafe person, and they also give suggestions about fixing the matter if you prove to be unsafe.

If Lorrie isn't speaking to a safe person, we will experience constant problems with communication. I must create a safe environment, and if she doesn't feel safe in the environment we have, I need to ask her, "What would it take for you to feel comfortable with our communications?" And I need to fix whatever is wrong.

This is just as important for men as it is for women. We men must also feel safe in our communications. Otherwise, marriage becomes a combat zone in which the partners are constantly firing at each other.

The Scriptures say:

The good man brings good things out of the good stored up in his heart, and the evil man brings evil things out of the evil stored up in his heart. For out of the overflow of his heart his mouth speaks. Luke 6:45

Again, what is inside shows forth during our communications.

Superficiality

Another communication blocker is superficiality. Why am I so afraid to let you see who I really am? Most of us want to know who the other person is, don't we?

It is so critical that we not have to live behind masks.

John Powell, a Jesuit priest, wrote an interesting book on this subject entitled *Why Am I Afraid to Tell You Who I Am?*[9] The answer is that if I tell you who I am, I don't have anything left. So, instead, I put on a mask. If you don't like that mask, I put on another one. And I keep putting on new masks until I find one you do like.

Putting on masks is easy, but unzipping my exterior façade and letting you see who I am is somehow difficult. If you see who I am and don't like it, and the result is that you make fun of me, run me down, or otherwise ridicule me, I will be devastated. If I am still afraid to tell you who I am, then it must mean that you have not yet created a safe atmosphere in which I can open up.

It is so critical that we not have to live behind masks. At some point, we must become willing to say, "Okay, I'll let you in so that you can see who I really am."

A critical point came in our relationship one day when Lorrie and I were talking in a restaurant in Alexandria, Virginia. I was saying to her, "I really like deep communication, and *this* is deep."

"It doesn't feel deep to me," she answered. As it turned out, for her, deep communication had to have visible emotion attached to it.

"This is deep," I protested, but I knew that for her to hear me, I had to let her see the emotion of pain. "Okay," I said to myself, here goes the shade, and I opened up and let her see me as I really was.

We have to say, "You want to see? Okay, here's what I look like on the inside. Here's who I am. Here's what I struggle with. Here's my pain." We must reach this point because it is impossible to experience the depths of intimacy until we are willing to remove the superficiality. The shade must go up, and we must let each other in.

Once my shade was up, I learned to live with it up most of the time and not yank it back down every time I felt threatened. Sometimes, in our own arrogance and pride, we think that we've opened ourselves up, but all we've done is taken off just one of the many filters that cover the real us. There are many more yet to come off.

The same is true with our relationship with God. The Bible speaks of a face-to-face relationship that He desires to have with us. All the shades must come off, so that we can see each other as we really are. It would be impossible to overemphasize this point.

If I am afraid to tell you who I am, it is because I don't trust you, and if I don't trust you, how far can we get in our relationship? When I am able to trust you, I will let you see who I am.

If Lorrie doesn't yet trust me and won't let me see inside of her, what will it take to create a safe place for her to open up? I must find the answer to that question and put it into operation if our relationship is to be what God intended it to be.

The Critical Mouth

Another communication blocker is the critical mouth. Words that tear down a person never correct a problem; they only intensify it, and in the process they further lower the self-esteem of the other person. It seems to be our human nature to think that if we can run the other person down that will somehow make us look better, but it's not true. All it does is make us look like an absolute jerk.

A saying that I heard many years ago goes like this:

> *Words, like weapons, ask no questions as they kill.*
> *People wounded once dancing now are standing still.* [20]

It's so true.

Most of us, at one time or another, have gotten so fired up that we drove in the arrow, stuck in the knife, and fired all the guns at our disposal, and then, for just a moment, we felt very proud of ourselves—as if we had accomplished something really great. That is … until we saw the crumpled heap on the floor and realized what we had really done—wounded the person we love. Then we were devastated and sorry.

Many of us, as we were growing up, used the old saying:

Sticks and stones may break my bones,
But words will never hurt me.

It was a lie then, and it's a lie now. In fact, it's a lie from the very pits of Hell. Nothing can hurt more than unkind words.

This is especially true if we are good at the war of words (and many of us are). We know just which weapon to choose and just where to thrust it so that the maximum damage is done. God never intended for words to be used in this way.

Defensiveness

Defensiveness is the greatest destroyer of communication. How do I know? Early in our marriage, I would defend my position at any cost. I was like Tom Sawyer when he said, "I will deny it for form's sake and stick to it from principle." But Lorrie didn't want to hear all the ninety reasons why I did what I did. She only wanted to hear that I was sorry or that I was willing to do it in a different way the next time.

Often couples engage in arguments that have very little to do with the discussion. One couple argued in my office over whether the hot dog they bought at the Pepsi Center cost $2.40 or $3.50. And each one defended their position. But what difference did it make? We need to stick to the issue at hand and not get sidetracked with unimportant matters.

When you have a tendency to become defensive, simply remember these words: "What is it that you need from me right now?" That kind of care will keep you from needing to defend your opinion—however "right" you may be.

Poor Eye Contact

Another communication blocker is the use of shifting eyes. Since 55 percent of every message is nonverbal, the look in the eyes says everything.

As I noted once before in this book, I am what is called "polyphasic." That is, I can concentrate on more than one thing at once. I can listen to television and read a book at the same time. But when I speak with Lorrie, she doesn't want me to be reading a book or watching television. It's not enough for me to say, "I'm listening." If my eyes are not on her, she cannot know that I'm listening.

Let people know that they have your full attention, and then you can have a fruitful conversation. If there is a television set on, turn it off so that you can talk properly without disturbance.

An Overtalking and Nagging Mouth

This is self-explanatory. The mouth of some people never seems to stop. This is known as "overtalk." Many times, what comes out of such a mouth is a lot of nagging.

Norm Wright, a respected Christian author on the subject of relationships, once gave a definition of nagging on one of his videos I enjoyed a lot. He said that nagging was a lot like being nibbled to death by a duck. I could somehow picture that.

But what is nagging all about? Someone came up with a rule called the 90/10 Rule, and I like it. They said, in essence, that there is 10 percent of any person that we don't like. I think that's probably true. There are things about me that other people (including Lorrie) don't like, and there are things about Lorrie that other people (including me) don't like. If the two of us concentrated on the 10 percent the other one can't stand, we would probably be driven mad.

But there is 90 percent of Lorrie that is absolutely incredible, and she thinks the same of me. As long as we can stick within that 90 percent, we're as happy as we can be.

Say to the nagging tongue, "Forget about the 10 percent of me you don't like, and concentrate on the 90 percent you do like."

I love the scripture that says:

Don't talk too much, for it fosters sin. Be sensible and turn off the flow!
Proverbs 10:19 NLT

The Living Bible says it like this:

Don't talk so much, you keep putting your foot in your mouth. Proverbs 10:19 TLB

The wise King Solomon wrote:

A fool's voice is known by multitude of words. Ecclesiastes 5:3 KJV

The words of the *New Living Translation* are much more colorful:

Being a fool makes you a blabbermouth. Ecclesiastes 5:3 NLT

If you are guilty of talking too much, learn to discipline your tongue and to spend more time listening.

4. Empathize with the Position of Your Mate

The fourth rule for having a healthy family fight is to empathize with your mate. Perception is everything, and if your mate senses that you are empathetic to them, it will change the atmosphere of your communication.

Empathy is having the ability to take off my glasses and put on Lorrie's glasses, so that I can see the world as she sees it and know where she is coming from. In the same way, she needs the ability to take off her glasses and put on mine, so that she can see the world as I see it.

When I empathize with you, it means not only that I understand how you view the world; it also means that I understand your pain, and I understand why you have it. Therefore, I understand your position.

Try this sometime: When you are having an argument, get up and change chairs, and begin to argue the other person's point. That's really an eye opener. As you argue their case, you gain insight into how they think, what is going on behind their eyes.

In the ideal marriage, each of you is a part of an arch. If one part of the arch is not complete, the structure will collapse. Learn to support each other.

Each of us sees the world in a very different light. One person, upon entering a room, notices a table with a plate and two bottles of water on it, and that's how they remember the room. To another, the very same room may look quite different. A third person may have an entirely different memory of the room. Each is valid and must not be discounted out of hand.

In the marriage, it takes both partners to gain a greater picture of the whole. I can see only so much, and that's my perception of the world. Lorrie can see only so much, and that's her perception of the world. Neither of us is wrong. We just have different perceptions, and if we can put our two perceptions together, we have a larger picture of the true world around us.

That's how we learn to manage our differences. Lorrie realizes that I'm not stupid, and I realize that she's not stupid, but that we just look at things differently.

Lorrie and I have completely different approaches to beaches, for example. I immediately want to walk along the beach, and she wants to just sit and enjoy the atmosphere. To my way of thinking, it seems stupid to have miles of beach and not be walking along it, and to her way of thinking, it seems stupid to have the calm of the beach and not sit and enjoy it.

The fact that two have become "one flesh" enriches both our worlds.

When we came to the place that I no longer tried to convince her that sitting on the beach was wrong, and she no longer tried to convince me that walking on the beach was wrong, we began to understand each other. Now, we sit for a while, and then we walk for a while. In this way, we enjoy the best of two worlds.

The fact that two have become *"one flesh"* enriches both our worlds. Now we have the advantage of two sets of eyes, both with peripheral and depth perception, joined together in their view of the world around them. This gives us a more balanced view.

Learn to empathize with the position of your mate.

5. Don't Bring Up the Past

The fifth rule for having a healthy family fight is not to bring up the past. Deal with the past by forgiving it.

As we have seen in Chapter One, Jesus taught: *"If you do not forgive men their sins, your Father will not forgive your sins"* (Matthew 6:15). Those who refuse to forgive place themselves outside the flow of God's grace. If you want

God's blessing on your life, then you must forgive your mate. This is critical. You must forgive all the issues of the past before you can move forward.

Then, establish effective boundaries to be used with each other. Lorrie and I had to learn this. For instance, she had the habit of standing at the top of the stairs and calling, "Darling…" or "Larry …" and then she waited for me to come upstairs to see what she wanted. That didn't feel good to me. I didn't like being "summoned." One day I said to her, "That doesn't work for me. You can call for me from upstairs, but I don't want to have to go all the way up just to see what you want." One day she called for me, and when I didn't come, she came downstairs and asked if I had heard her. "I heard you," I answered with a smile, "but I wasn't coming."

She had things that I did that bothered her, and she had to make those things clear to me so that I could understand and not do them anymore. In that way, rather than hold grudges against each other, we came to understand each other's viewpoint, and we could forgive and manage the process.

One man was a CPA, and since he was the sole breadwinner in the family he insisted that both he and his wife be very careful with their money. He, on the other hand, had the habit of breaking things when he got angry. That didn't work well for her, so she told him that he could break things if he wanted, but she would replace them with the best items she could find and charge them on his credit card.

One day when he got upset about something, he took off his watch, threw it on the garage floor, and stomped on it. "That's fine," she said, when she saw it, and then she went out and bought a thirteen-hundred-dollar watch and charged it on his credit card.

The next time he became angry about something, he drove his fist through the wall of the guest bathroom. She responded by bringing in an interior decorator and having the guest bathroom completely done over. And she charged it all on his credit card.

One day he picked up the remote control for the television, threw it against the wall, and broke it to pieces. She went out and bought the most expensive replacement she could find and charged it to his credit card.

After about a half dozen of these experiences, he finally began to change, deciding that the consequences of his actions were too great.

A system of boundaries and consequences can easily be created within a healthy relationship. Set the boundaries, learn to forgive, and then move on to greater things.

6. Understand Your Differences

The sixth rule for having a healthy family fight is to be aware of and understand your differences. Neither of you is wrong. Your answers to the same question may be different, but you just have two right answers. Therefore, the task is learning to manage your differences.

If you insist, "You're wrong to try to parent like you do," or "You're wrong to spend money the way you do," you have created a confrontation between one person who is right and another who is wrong. In every conflict then, there must be a winner and a loser, so you have one winner and one loser every time. As I have noted, this is not healthy.

If you lived by yourself, that might work, but in marriage, you can't afford to do that. You and your spouse are one unit, and you must live for each other. If you are always right, and they are always wrong, there can be no intimacy. When you place each other at opposite ends of an argument, you are no longer lovers, but opponents in a battle of life. If you're not careful, you'll find yourself "sleeping with the enemy." Learn what your differences are and how to manage them.

A fun exercise we have used sometimes in our marriage seminars is to ask each spouse to describe the color blue. To one, blue might be one shade, and to the other, blue might be (or probably will be) an entirely different shade. Neither of you is wrong, and both of you are right. All blues are blue, even though they are quite different. One of you may like one particular blue, and to you, that's what blue is. But the other is not wrong to prefer another blue. Just because your opinion differs, that doesn't make you wrong. You're both right, so learn to appreciate the differences of opinion and to respect them, rather then ridicule them.

If you, as a parent, are strict with your children, and you see them turning out to be angels, that doesn't mean that the approach of the other is necessarily wrong. Each child is different and needs to be approached differently. Learn to appreciate the divergent points of view on child raising and learn to parent together. Often, it is the balance of two very different approaches that proves effective.

Lorrie and I could not seem to agree on how to handle the fact that our son Jared left his things lying around all the time, and we wrestled with the issue for many days. I wanted to do one thing, and she wanted to do something very different. I didn't like her approach, and she didn't like mine.

Eventually we settled upon a solution that seemed rather absurd to both of us. When we found anything belonging to our son lying around, we would put it in a big box in the closet. We told him of our decision, and then we began to implement it.

That solved the problem. Lorrie didn't have to drag Jared's things all over the house, she didn't have to get upset about it ever again, and so it was no longer a point of contention between us.

And it also helped Jared. Anything he was looking for was "in the box." His homework went in there, diet coke cans went in there, his uneaten pie went in there, and his football equipment went in there. Before long, the whole thing got to be very funny.

Lorrie and I had found a way to put this problem in context. I was not right and her wrong, and she was not right and me wrong. We were both right, and we found a way to compromise on the issue that put the pressure where it belonged—on Jared.

We had first thought of piling everything onto his bed, but since it wasn't possible to have a sort of laundry chute that would drop things from every room in the house directly onto his bed, we settled on the box. And that worked well.

Stop demanding that every family member think like you. It won't happen, so learn to manage your differences.

7. Express Your Feelings Truthfully

The seventh rule for having a healthy family fight is to express your feelings truthfully. In the midst of our conflict, we are often unwilling to tell each other exactly what we are feeling. We should be able to do that, to do it without anger, and to feel safe in doing it.

What are you really thinking? What am I really thinking? Are we just dancing round the real issues? I had to learn all of this.

I remember lying next to Lorrie in bed so afraid to bring up the issues that were bothering me that I wondered if my heartbeat would wake her up and get her attention. It is sometimes hard to remember those days now, and it doesn't make sense to me that it happened, but I know that it did and that many other people suffer the same limitations. It takes courage in the midst of all of our conflict to say, "There's something that's really bothering me, and I hope we can talk about it."

If you are telling your spouse that they have hurt you, do it with great care not to hurt them in return.

We must strike a balance here. Some people pride themselves on being so blunt that they hurt everyone around them. "Boy, I told them!" they boast. That's not the idea. The idea is to express your feelings, not at the expense of your mate, but while respecting their feelings.

If you are telling your spouse that they have hurt you, do it with great care not to hurt them in return. Your purpose in telling them must not be to hurt them back, but to improve your communications and thus improve your intimacy.

"When you _____ , I feel _____ ," should be a legitimate statement in any marriage and can be expressed inoffensively and lovingly. "When you _____ , I feel embarrassed," for instance.

Lorrie was very critical of the way I drove on snow and ice. It left her unsettled. I was perfectly calm because I had never had an accident on snow or ice, but to her way of thinking I was driving recklessly. That was very difficult for me to understand.

One day she was able to express herself better. Rather than accuse me of driving recklessly, she said that she felt afraid when I drove as I did on snow and ice. Suddenly a bell went off in my brain. I didn't want to do anything that caused her to be afraid, and I was willing to do anything to keep that from happening. This changed the way I drove, but it didn't happen because she accused me of being a reckless driver, but because she made me understand how my driving in severe weather made her feel.

If a mate is clowning around, and you don't like it, don't just criticize them for their behavior. Tell them how embarrassing it is to you and explain to them why. Give them a reason to change. "If it embarrasses you, then I won't do it again," will usually be their response. Instead of stabbing them in the back, you have given them a reason to improve their behavior.

Spouses are not mind readers, like we wish they were. We have to tell each other what is bothering us. In this way, we help each other improve. If we do it in a wrong way or with a wrong attitude, things just may get worse instead of better, and we just might drive a permanent wedge between us.

And just because you said it once several years ago doesn't mean that your spouse will always remember. Be willing to reinforce what you have said at times if need be. Without being obnoxious, repeat it as often as necessary.

Learn to express your feelings truthfully.

8. Set a Limit on the Amount of Time You Spend Discussing Problems

The eighth rule for having a healthy family fight is to set a limit on the amount of time you're willing to spend discussing problems. Your marriage should never become a continual round of conflict resolution. Take a break from the heavy stuff. Lighten up. Some people can discuss issues to death. Set limits. You need times that are just for enjoyment and acceptance.

Take time to have fun. Plan a date night. Personally, I think that you should do it once a week, the same night every week if possible. Lorrie and I have had a date night every week now for twenty-three years, and, yes, that's longer than we have been married. It's because we started this custom when we were just dating. But don't stop dating once you are married. Set aside some nights for a special date.

As we have noted, date night is not a time to work on resolving conflicts in the marriage, and it's not a time to sit together at home and watch television. Do something fun together that will help you advance your relationship.

You know what is fun for you, so do it. Have a good meal together, and while you are doing it, talk about things you like. Enjoy each other. Build your friendship.

I often prescribe a weekend away for hurting couples. During that time, I warn them, they are not to talk about money matters, their work, or their children. Often they look at me like I'm crazy. How can they avoid those issues? What else do they have in common?

And that's the problem. Set times and places each week for conflict resolution. That's important. But also have a date night when you refuse to discuss any differences and just enjoy each other—like you did before you were married.

You might want to have breakfast together every Saturday morning or meet somewhere on a particular day for lunch. Make it a very special time for the both of you.

Set a limit on the amount of time you spend discussing problems.

9. Solve Problems Now Rather Than Later

The ninth rule for having a healthy family fight is to solve problems now rather than later. When problems arise, seek to resolve them then. Don't wait. Delays only tend to add to the resentment and the confusion. If you wait for very long, you will have five issues to deal with rather than just one, and that makes it much harder to resolve.

Learn to deal with problems as soon after they occur as possible. That doesn't mean that you jump on your mate at eleven o'clock at night. As soon as possible means as soon as practical, as soon as it is convenient for the both of you. If it is late at night when the problem arises, the next day is soon enough to discuss it.

10. Allow Time for Change

The tenth rule for having a healthy family fight is to allow time for change. Old habits supported by old ways of thinking require time to change. You will not change with the snap of a finger, and you can't expect others to change that fast either. Patience is a virtue.

At the same time, it shouldn't take five years to change. Let your spouse see some progress in you, and they will be more inclined to be patient with you as you change. And expect to see some progress in your spouse.

11. Agreed-Upon Solutions Are Not Forever

The eleventh rule for having a healthy family fight is to know that agreed-upon solutions are not forever. Some of us want to lock everything in, to set it in concrete, so that it can never again be changed. That's just not possible in human relationships. Try something for a while, and then see if it's working for you. If it's not, go back to the drawing board and try to come up with something better.

Always provide your mate with the courtesy of being able to return to the negotiating table if some agreed-upon solution is no longer working.

"But we agreed!" one or the other wants to insist. Maybe so, but if what we agreed upon isn't working, why stick with it forever? That would be crazy.

The problem here is very much like the original conflict. Whatever it is may not be working for one of the mates, but the other one cannot insist, "It's working fine for me," and ignore their spouse's complaint. If it is not working well for one mate—regardless of the reasons—then another solution is needed. Don't fight it. Agreed-upon solutions are not forever.

12. Learn to Recognize Developmental Crises

The twelfth rule for having a healthy family fight is to learn to recognize developmental crises. There are certain times in our relationship when things happen that cause crises. We must learn to recognize these and deal with them before they do us permanent damage.

Some of them are easily recognizable. When a pregnancy occurs in the family, for instance, all sorts of new stresses are experienced. Many things will have to change. Children can be a lot of fun, and having a child can do a lot of good for a marriage, but the process of having the child and then caring for the child over many long years puts a relationship under new and sometimes unexpected stresses. For one, both parents suddenly experience fatigue because of not sleeping regular hours, and this makes them irritable.

By the time my son came along, my first wife and I had lived a long time together without anyone else. One night we actually left the house together and forgot that we had him. We had to turn around and go back for him.

Job changes and moving from one place to another can often be stressful on everyone, and this creates conflict. No one is to blame. It just happens.

The changes that wives experience during a monthly cycle commonly cause many problems in marriage and family life. No one is to blame, so no shouting and accusation is in order. We just need to recognize what is causing the problem and learn to deal with it before it escalates into something more serious.

As I noted previously in this book, Lorrie and I agreed to just coast through her times of PMS (meaning that we refused to discuss serious issues such as money matters or issues involving the children during those days). If we tried, it invariably led to even more conflict.

Before we learned this, life was something of a mystery at those times of the month. After several days of conflict, I would be feeling bloodied from battle, and she would suddenly become playful. "What is going on?" I wondered. Thank goodness, we eventually learned.

This was all no one's fault, and we learned to recognize that fact and move on. If anyone was to blame, it was the hormones.

In the same way, Lorrie learned to recognize times of particular stress for me and to give me more slack during those times. She gave me a wider berth, so to speak, and didn't call me on everything I was saying and doing.

Being part of a stepfamily presents a whole new series of issues, and these affect our conduct. It's no one's fault. The problems are just there, so we have to learn to deal with them.

Learn to recognize developmental crises.

13. Lovemaking Is No Way To Deal with Conflict

The thirteenth rule for having a healthy family fight is that lovemaking is not a way to deal with conflict. Dealing with conflicts is, itself, in conflict with an act of lovemaking. This would seem to be obvious, but some people unwisely use lovemaking as a bridge to solve some conflict or other.

Using lovemaking as a means of celebration when a conflict is finally settled can be a way to restore closeness when feelings are back to normal. But never use it as a way to resolve the conflict itself.

How to Go About Improving Your Communication

It has been said that 95 percent of the conflicts you will face in life—with a colleague at work, with spouse and/or children at home, or with a friend—

are caused by a miscommunication or an abuse of communication. Think about this when you communicate with others.

It took Lorrie and me a number of years to get all of these techniques working for us, so don't feel defeated if you don't get everything working at once. Take one or two of these issues, discuss them with your spouse, and together figure out how you can improve your relationship. If you try to address too many things at once, you may become overwhelmed.

"Thirteen things! We'll never get them all right!" Just take baby steps at first, and soon, before you know it, you'll be walking on water.

The last thing I would say about all of this is to pray. Prayer is the very highest form of communication, and it will change things for you. Ask God to show you the things that need to be changed in you and to help you change them, and to show your spouse the things that need to be changed in them and to help them change them. He can help you do that as no one else can.

Since communication is not something that comes automatically for most of us, and we were not born good communicators and good listeners, ask the Lord to help you. When you begin working to eliminate the conflicts in your relationship, you will remove all sorts of barriers that are keeping you from better things.

Finally, check your mate periodically to see if everything is okay. Put your arms around them and ask them if anything is bothering them. Ask them how you're doing as their spouse, and don't be offended by their response. Ask them if there is anything you need to talk over, anything you need to address to make them more at ease with the relationship. If you don't ask, how can you know?

If you have resolved all of your issues, but your spouse has not, you're still not okay as a couple. If one of you has a problem, both of you have the problem. Deal with it, so that you can live happily ever after.

Those Dreadful Money Matters

(Or How to Effectively Manage the Family Finances)

Whoever loves money never has money enough. Ecclesiastes 5:10

*I*sn't this an interesting statement? If we go through life chasing money, we will never have enough of it. The person who loves wealth is never satisfied with his income—no matter how large it becomes. It is only when we can get away from the focus on money that we can find satisfaction and contentment in who we are and what life has dealt us, and then we can learn to make the best of it.

The Scriptures also say:

For the love of money is a root of all kinds of evil. Some people, eager for money, have wandered from the faith and pierced themselves with many griefs. 1 Timothy 6:10

Money is not evil in itself; it is *"a root"* of evil, it is one of the greatest motivators—for bad or for good—and it is at the core of many marital conflicts. If we are to have the relationship God intended, we must bring the financial aspects of our relationship into balance, and this requires that we learn and put into operation certain principles of budgeting. After all, if we don't tell our money where we *want* it to go, we will end up wondering where it has all gone.

Someone has said that spendthrifts and tightwads often marry each other, and there seems to be an element of truth in this. There is always one marriage partner who seems to be more conservative when it comes to spending money, and the other partner usually wants to spend more. Oddly, the conservative partner usually likes the liberalism of the other mate, and the liberal mate usually prefers that the more conservative person be in charge of the family funds. It's not that they like this arrangement, but they agree that it's for the best. This seems to bring a good balance into the marriage.

The marriages that get into trouble quickly are those in which both partners are liberal spenders. They agree that they need new furniture, that the house needs immediate redecorating, and that they must have a vacation, and they drag out the credit cards to pay for all of it. Neither of them stops to think that there is no money to pay the bill when it comes due. This is dangerous.

There are some basic philosophies that we all need to develop concerning money.

Holding Your Money Together

In the marriage, it is very dangerous to have "his money" and "her money." If money, whatever its source, does not become "our money," it will probably cause problems between us. Put all the money into one pot, and then learn how to spend it well.

Some choose to keep their money separate, but this is often an indication that they have not resolved differences over money issues. And it is not an acceptable solution. Money kept apart will inevitably become the cause of a disagreement. It happens every time.

If you insist on keeping your money separate, then you are essentially two single people living together, and that won't work. Before long, you'll be screaming at each other over some money matter or other.

One couple that visited me for counseling insisted that they were successfully holding their money separately, but they were already screaming at each other before they left my office. He wasn't happy with the fact that she wasn't putting any money into retirement (as he was), and she wasn't happy with the fact that he refused to help with the children's school clothing (although it was the end of summer and the beginning of the new school year).

Also, when you hold your money separately, you feel more free to do things without first consulting your mate, and that must not be done in any marriage.

Did you get married? You may indeed have a piece of paper that proclaims you are legally joined. But are you now *"one"*? If so, then act like it. Keeping your money in separate accounts seems to indicate that you are still two single people doing your own thing under the guise of a marriage certificate. The worst case I had to deal with was that man who had sold a car to his wife. That's about as bad as it gets.

If you insist on keeping your money separate, then you are essentially two single people living together, and that won't work.

The Proper Use of Credit

Every family must develop a philosophy concerning the buying on credit. The use of credit is so liberal these days and is so pervasive in society that it has become dangerous to young couples. It is very easy to get over your head in debt quickly, and that can adversely affect your relationship.

How does easy credit affect us? If you have a ten-dollar bill in your pocket, and you go shopping for an anniversary present, how much will you spend? That's easy, isn't it? You'll spend ten dollars. If, on the other hand, you go shopping for an anniversary present, and you have a credit card with you, how much will you be likely to spend? You will probably find something you really like, and you will spend as much as it costs. After all, you don't have to pay for it until next month—or you can even extend the payment. This is one of the greatest dangers credit cards present. They give us a false sense of how much we can spend and how much we are spending—whether or not we can afford it.

When we first accept the use of a credit card, our thought is that it will be only for emergencies. But why is it that so many emergencies suddenly present themselves that our credit limit is quickly consumed?

Before the use of credit became so widespread, we had to do everything by cash, and consequently we found ways to spend less. When the tires wore out on our cars, for example, we sometimes found good tires at a junkyard very cheap. Now that we buy our tires with a credit card and can pay later, why bother? New tires are always better, or at least that's what we tell ourselves.

In this way, easy credit has totally changed the American lifestyle. Families suffer the consequences down the road as bills come due and the entire family budget is strained to meet them.

When I was nineteen, I landed a good job as the circulation manager for a newspaper. The head of the print shop was a man named James Mouser, and I wish I had listened to James. One day he said to me, "Larry, don't fall into the credit trap. Try not to get a bunch of credit cards."

"James," I said with an air of knowing, "credit is just the American way. Buying things on credit and then being able to pay them off in small payments is what has made America great." And I proceeded to plunge into the credit trap.

I bought some new furniture. It only cost me $400, and I could pay for it over time. So I was very proud of myself.

But I was only earning $1.25 an hour, and it took me so long to pay off that $400 that it might as well have been the national debt.

When my first wife and I separated for the first time and suddenly I found myself living alone, I wanted to change my life dramatically. "If I'm going to have to sit in this house by myself," I thought, "I'm going to have some nice things." I went out to Montgomery Wards and bought a vibrating and heating recliner and a nice color television with a remote control, and they only cost me $52 a month. But as time wore on, it seemed that I would be paying $52 a month for the rest of my life. I thought I was never going to get that debt paid off, and by the time I did, the remote control no longer worked, nor the heating option on the recliner. I needed to learn to use credit wisely, and I needed to learn it fast.

Credit cards are dangerous. Should we own one or more of them or not? It's a question each of us has to answer for ourselves.

When Lorrie and I met, she had fourteen credit cards. We agreed that this was dangerous, and one day we cut up all of her credit cards except two and threw them away. We decided that we would keep a few credit cards (for the

124

convenience) but that we would pay them off every month and that we would never again fall into the credit trap, because if you're carrying large balances on your credit cards, you can quickly get into serious financial difficulty.

Well, there was a problem with those cut-up credit cards. We had thrown them away, but we didn't think about the need to close the accounts themselves. They were still there tempting us. Whenever Lorrie had the desire to buy something, she would remember one of those accounts and attempt to charge items on them.

Stores were only too cooperative. They had the information on file, and it would just pop up when they entered her name. They didn't care if she had the original card or not. They were eager to honor the account anyway. So take a lesson from that. When you cut up a credit card, remember to also close the corresponding account.

There is another good rule to follow when cutting up credit cards. Dispose of one part in the trash in one room and the other part in the trash in another room. That way, the two parts of the card will not somehow get back together again and decide to remarry.

Allowances

For many years, I resisted the idea of budgeting my money. "I don't have enough money to budget," I insisted. "If everything we earn goes to pay bills, why have a budget? What possible good would it do?"

Underneath all of my excuses was the reality that I did not want to be accountable to anyone for what I spent. I wanted to spend what I wanted to spend, and I didn't want anyone asking questions about it. After all, I was an adult now, and I didn't need anyone's permission to spend my hard-earned money.

When Lorrie and I sought a means of controlling our spending and agreed to budget everything, we then came up with the idea of allowances for each other. We would each receive a certain amount of money each paycheck, and we wouldn't have to give an account to anyone for what we spent from that allowance. This seemed to work for us.

We still get an allowance today—$50 each paycheck or $100 a month. (We started out at $15 each paycheck, $30 a month, many years ago.) We spend it as we want, and no accounting is required.

Once Lorrie took a class on how to be a clown, and she had to buy the most awful shoes for her clown's outfit. She paid $100 for those shoes. When I knew about it, I asked, "Why are you spending a hundred dollars on these?"

"What's it to you?" she was able to say, "It's out of my allowance." And that ended the conversation. If she wants to, she can buy ugly shoes with her allowance.

I can accumulate my allowance and then go to my favorite toy stores—Radio Shack and Sharper Image, and I can buy whatever I want, without checking first with Lorrie. It's my money.

If I want to, I can buy my wife something nice with that money, or I can buy something for the children. However, there is no expectation that I spend it on them. I also don't have to spend it on myself. If I want to, I can give the money away, and no one will question me about it. We sometimes call it our "play money." This custom provides some little freedom for us, and it is the only freedom we have allowed ourselves in this area.

Lorrie has no right to say to me, "If you really loved me, you would spend that allowance on me." The flowers I buy her don't come out of my allowance, the birthday presents I buy her don't come out of my allowance, and the groceries I buy for the house don't come out of my allowance.

If we're out of money at the moment, and we want to go out to eat, sometimes I'll say, "Let's go out anyway, and I'll pay the tab out of my allowance." That's my choice. Later, I can't go back and get a reimbursement from general funds. If I spent my allowance, then I spent it, but I can choose to spend it on whatever I want to spend it on.

My allowance is not for gasoline for the car, it's not for buying coffee, and it's not for taking a friend to lunch. It's mine to spend as I want, and Lorrie and I like that little freedom.

Lorrie squirrels her allowance money away in a little box. I'm never sure where she has hidden it because she moves it around so that I can't find it. That's okay. It's her money.

This is the only time in our house that we ever have a "mine" and "yours" label on anything. An allowance may be one item you will want to introduce into your budget.

One of the issues we had to resolve concerning allowances was whether or not the person earning more at the moment should be entitled to a larger allowance. Who earned the most seesawed back and forth between the two of us a number of times in the years to come, but it just so happened that when we established our system of allowances Lorrie was earning more than I was. Because she was earning more, she felt that she was entitled to more allowance. We talked this over and came to the conclusion that it was not a good idea because money often leads to power struggles within the marriage, and we wanted to prevent that at any cost. The person earning the most money should not be the most powerful person in the family simply because of income. This decision simplified the issue of allowances.

A real savings account is one in which you put money in and leave it in.

Savings

Many Americans keep a savings account, but it is a savings account in name only. They deposit money into it each month, but they also withdraw money from it each month. In this way, it's a sort of glorified checking account. They call it a savings account, but the account never has much money in it. A real savings account is one in which you put money in and leave it in. That's why it is called savings. You are saving it for some future time.

I recommend that couples save and that they begin with a budgeted item of at least 1 percent of their income and build it up gradually until they have reached 10 percent. In this way, you will be using 10 percent of your income for God (more on this later) and 10 percent for yourselves. Save that 10 percent of your income for a rainy day.

In one of the premarital counseling classes I was teaching I asked the question, "How would you like to have 10 percent of everything you've ever earned?" A man came to me later and said, "I am that man. I have saved 10 percent of everything I ever earned."

He was not then engaged to be married, but was only attending the class because he had a desire to prepare for marriage in the future. A single lady who was also attending the class overheard what he said that day, and she was so impressed with it that she married him.

127

Unfortunately, this story did not have a happy ending. As it turned out, the man had 10 percent of everything he had ever earned for a reason. He was as tightfisted as anyone I had ever seen. He didn't want to spend on anything. This failing eventually destroyed their marriage.

When I counsel couples to save, I'm not advocating tightfistedness. I'm referring to a reasonable and rational savings, giving some thought to the future.

Thinking about the future is not incompatible with the belief that God will always provide for us. It is a means in which God provides for us for a time when our earning power has declined, some unforeseen emergency arises, or some sudden opportunity comes to us that we have not anticipated and therefore have not provided for.

Do whatever you can to make your future secure and trust God for the rest. If the stock market suddenly dies at some point, then you will lose anything you have invested there. But, in the meantime, you will have done whatever you could to make your future secure.

God requires that of us. He steps in at the limit of our capabilities, but He expects us to go as far as we can on what He has given us. Then we will depend on trust.

Money for Emergencies

It is wise for every family to have an emergency fund. What happens if the engine or the transmission of your car goes out? These are major expense items. What happens when your old faithful refrigerator suddenly quits on you? Other emergencies might be a natural disaster of some kind, a health emergency or a death in the family. Most of us, because we have not saved, are forced at this point to go deeper into debt. A fund set aside for this purpose would help to avoid that eventuality.

When certain emergencies have arisen in our lives, Lorrie and I have looked at each other and said, "Thank God we had this little nest egg we can fall back on." It saved the day. We were not angry to see it go. We were just thankful that we had accumulated it. And then we started working on another emergency fund to replace it.

This isn't to say that in times of emergency we don't remember the promise of Malachi:

I will prevent pests from devouring your crops, and the vines in your fields will not cast their fruit. Malachi 3:11

Or as the *King James Version* of the Bible puts it:

I will rebuke the devourer for your sakes.

We must do all that is within our own possibilities, and then we can believe God to *"rebuke the devourer for* [our] *sakes."*

Money for Travel

Lorrie and I love to travel, so we developed the habit of accumulating a little travel fund. Most American families love to take vacations—even if it's only a camping trip to the mountains, but too many wait until the last moment to think about the money needed for such a trip. When you charge a vacation, it seems to take forever to pay for it. Make your needed vacation money a regular item in your monthly budget.

How will you decide how much you need to budget for vacations? If you plan to spend two thousand dollars on a vacation next summer or fall, for instance, give yourself ten or eleven months to accumulate it. That's about two hundred dollars a month. If you can't afford that much, then you shouldn't plan to take such a costly vacation.

Lorrie and I also have what we call our getaway fund. We like to go away together for a few days every quarter, and I highly recommend this habit to all married couples. Sometimes we just go across town to a nice hotel running a weekend special. Search for some bargains in your area.

Sometimes you may want to go to the mountains or, at other times, to the beach. Go camping together, or occasionally, go somewhere exotic together for a special treat. Search for the best rates.

Again, during these special moments, you won't want to be concerned with talking about your children, about your finances, or about your work. This is a fun time to build your relationship and enjoy each other. If that sounds good to you, plan for it, and save for it.

Money for Christmas

Why is it that Christmas always seems to surprise us, and we're not ready for it? If you haven't noticed, Christmas comes at the same time every year. About the 10th of December, it suddenly hits us that it's almost here again, and we desperately try to get some money together. Far too many of us charge everything about Christmas, and we're still paying this Christmas off when next Christmas rolls around.

I recommend the formation of a Christmas club. Most credit unions have them, but if not, you can create your own. Put a certain amount of money in a designated account every month, and then when next Christmas comes around, you'll be ready for it—perhaps for the first time in your life.

Once you have a certain amount designated for Christmas spending, be careful not to go over that amount. Most of us go way overboard with Christmas, and it doesn't make the holiday any better at all. Spend what you have and no more, and then start saving for the next year.

How do you decide how much to budget for Christmas? Use the past few Christmases as a guide. Then, try to think ahead about how much you need to spend to have a nice Christmas for your family and friends, divide that into monthly payments, and then make them in advance.

Whatever you do, don't be guilty of getting so caught up in the activities of Christmas that you forget the real meaning of the season. Christmas is wonderful, but because of how much we spend on that holiday, January is the month most filled with depression and suicide in this country, and much of that is related to debt. People get overwhelmed by the hopelessness of never being able to pay it all back and maybe never again really having quite as nice a holiday season.

I make the radical suggestion to people that they not charge gifts at all. After all, if you charge it, you've lost the meaning of it. Gifts should represent something joyful and happy, not the heartache of having to repay huge consumer debts. Putting yourself into a financial jam to give a gift is not wise.

If you have to, make your gifts and/or your cards. Often a gift or a card made with your own hand will be even more appreciated than something you could buy, and you will avoid the credit trap. You can also do this for wedding gifts, anniversary gifts, and birthday gifts.

Gifts, aside from your Christmas club set aside, should form an item in your monthly budget: birthdays, anniversaries, the birth of babies, etc. Events such as these will continue to occur next year, and you need to prepare for them. Christmas is a big item and merits the special treatment, but also make allowance for other gifts as well.

Your Budget

Your budget is more than your house and car payments or your rent and utilities. If you only list those, you might seem to have a lot of money left over each month. But life is a lot more than house and car expenses. Include all of the various expenses you incur on a daily basis.

For instance, don't forget little things like your newspaper and magazine subscriptions, your eating out, and your entertainment. Little things can add up.

To many people, the idea of forming a budget seems almost as daunting as going to the moon and back. If you are one of those who keep meticulous records of everything, then you have it made. For everyone else, there's a relatively easy way to do it.

Find some sort of suitable box and place it in a convenient location where you can deposit in it all the receipts for expenses incurred for one month. Even if you spend money in cash, write it down on a small piece of paper and drop it into that box. Let's say, for example, that you spend twenty-five cents on a gumball. Write it down, and put it into the box. If you put money into a parking meter downtown, write it down and put it in the box. That's not too hard, is it?

Now, it gets a little more complicated, but not much. At the end of the month, take out the papers you have accumulated in the box and categorize them. By that I mean that you should sort them according to the type of expenditure they represent—gasoline, snacks, clothing, etc.—and add up the expenses for each category. Now you know how much you have spent and exactly where your money has gone. That's what a budget is all about.

Early in our marriage, money seemed to be disappearing fast. We had some money in savings, but it, too, was slipping away. Part of the problem proved to be the ATM machines that were just coming into their own.

Our children loved those ATM machines. After all, when you didn't have enough money, all you had to do was slip a little plastic card into the ATM machine, and out came more money. *Voila!* To the children, this seemed to be a never-ending supply of ready cash. Some children also think that checks can be written for any amount at any time, regardless of how much you have deposited in your account. Oh, that it were so!

Somehow we had to get a handle on our spending. We did what I have recommended here, using a Kleenex box to keep all of the receipts and slips of paper, and at the end of the next month we were amazed by the sum total of our expenditures.

For one thing, we were spending an incredible amount of money eating out, and we were also spending an incredible amount of money on food that we were bringing home to eat. If I remember right, we had spent nearly a thousand dollars that month just eating. No wonder our savings were dwindling! That was a huge amount of expenditure for that one item. Now we understood it and could work to get it under control.

It's amazing how many people have no idea how much they have spent and what they have spent it for. I worked with a nurse to develop a budget for her because she was having difficulty paying her bills on time. The budget showed that she would have only twenty-five dollars left over at the end of each month for discretionary spending. When she looked over the sum of her expenses, she said, "I knew it would be bad, but I had no idea it would be *this* bad." She'd had no idea what it was actually costing her to live.

How can we not know what we spend for? We need to know where our money is going. Then we can decide if we want to change any habits or not. And this is the way to start. When we see where we have been we can then decide where we want to go.

How much have you spent for gifts in recent months? The monthly average of that figure will become your monthly expense for gifts. What did you spend last year for Christmas? That amount, divided into twelve months, will become your monthly expense item for Christmas. Do this for each item of expenditure. And suddenly you know where you stand and what you can afford.

Money for Benevolence

Aside from all of our own personal needs and wants, we Christians believe in benevolence. First, we believe in tithing, or giving to God the first 10 percent of our increase. It is His, and it should come right off of the top of our income before anything else is spent.

Some may ask, "Well, should you tithe on your gross income or on the net?" Well, it depends. Someone has suggested that if you give a tithe of the gross income you will receive a gross blessing, and if you give a tithe of the net income, you will receive a net blessing. Clearly this is a decision each of us must make. It's between you and God. But, at the very least, you should be tithing from your earnings.

Every seed planted produces, and we cannot have a harvest without a planting.

An interesting thing happened to me once. Having applied for a job as a loan officer at a bank, I was interviewed by the bank president. He knew that I attended a local church and that I was active in that church, so he said he wanted to ask me a question. "What would happen," he said, "if you knew that someone from your church was paying their tithe, and they were behind on their pickup truck payment? Would you make it a point to tell them not to pay their tithe and to pay their pickup payment instead? Or would you have them pay their tithe and risk the repossession of their pickup truck?"

It was an interesting question, and I pondered it for a long time. I wasn't sure of the answer, but what I could say was that we should never allow ourselves to be put into a position of not paying our bills because that would bring shame to the cause of Christ. For our part, Lorrie and I have made a commitment to God to pay our tithes—100 percent—without fail for any reason. We have seen that God is faithful, and when we plant that seed in the ground, He always gives us a harvest, returning our seed to us with interest.

The tithe is the very least we can give to God, and above that most of us also feel called to give offerings. And we love to help other people when we can. This is a sign of our gratitude to God, and we do it willingly and joyfully.

Every seed planted produces, and we cannot have a harvest without a planting. That's why we look for opportunities to give, and I would recommend it to every believer. When you learn to give to God, you cannot fail to be blessed.

In recent years, it has been exciting for Lorrie and me to be able to give more money away than we spend paying our bills, and we're convinced that this is what God wants for each believing couple. There is no greater feeling than sowing seed back into His Kingdom and spending for His glory, and He wants you to experience that too. Every time you plant a seed in the ground, expect a harvest, for it will surely come.

Budget Billing

Should we use budget billing or not? This is the offer from utility companies to average out our expenditures with them over a year's period and charge that amount to us monthly, rather than having small bills come to us one month (in times of low usage) and a much larger one other months (in times of peak usage). If you exceed your consumption last year, it won't matter. The difference will be billed to you the following year in the same way.

Budget billing is sometimes done by the quarter or some other time period rather than a year, but the process is the same. This seems to us to be a wise thing to do. It helps you know up-front what your expenses will be each month during the next year. It certainly can't hurt anything.

Who Makes the Spending Decisions?

So who should make the spending decisions at your house? Since money matters are so divisive, both of you should have a part in making these decisions. They should be made together.

At one point, Lorrie and I were having a money meeting every Sunday night. I hated those meetings because I hated to talk about money. For Lorrie, it came very easy, but I was defensive about money.

I didn't want to talk about it. I didn't want to have to explain what I wanted to do or why I wanted to do it. And I didn't want to fight about money. Why couldn't we just live in peace and forget the money talks? But there were things we needed to talk about and agree upon.

We should never allow money matters to prevent us from living in peace and harmony, and yet more fights erupt in the marriage arena over money than over nearly any other subject you can imagine.

When I find couples at issue over money, I can usually know that there is a problem of trust in the marriage. Arguments about money are usually arguments about trust. If you handle money matters easily between you, it means that you trust each other. If there is a problem in this area, rather than sweep it under the rug and divide your money, it's best to deal with the trust issue between you. Whatever you do, learn to make all financial decisions together.

The Process of Establishing Financial Priorities

Many fights erupt because one or the other marriage partner has prepared a budget, and the other mate is not in agreement. For this reason, neither one of you should attempt to make a budget alone. This matter can be so explosive that it must be done in concert. This is the job for a committee.

Lorrie does not have the right to prepare a budget and simply present it to me for approval, and I also do not have that right. We do it together, and then there can be no complaints from either side.

Once the agreed-upon budget is in place, every financial decision hinges upon it. For years, I thought I might like to own a party barge, a pontoon-type boat complete with a little barbecue grill. You can swim off the side of them or relax onboard, and they are large enough to entertain quite a nice little group. I knew that Lorrie would never say no to me, but she would wisely reply, "Let's look at our budget and see how we can afford it." And that would settle the issue. We might have saved $20 a month and been able to afford the party barge by 2052, but, since the budget drives the train, that's the only way we could have done it.

If we hadn't had a budget, I might have imagined that I could afford a large party boat. It is the budget that reveals what we can and cannot afford. And, because we sit down together and lay out our priorities, that avoids the danger of one of us suddenly wanting something that we simply can't afford to buy.

This is not about who writes the checks. That's just a clerical function. This is about deciding where our money will and will not be spent. In our case, Lorrie writes all of our checks because it makes her feel safer to know that the bills are paid. I use a debit card for my purchases. Then I write "DEBIT CARD" across the top of the corresponding receipt and give it to her for recording in the checkbook.

At any time, I can open the checkbook and see what she has spent, she knows exactly what I have spent, and we talk about any resulting issues that arise. But our spending limits, in the form of the budget, are set ahead of time by mutual agreement.

A Good Budget Document

What exactly does a budget document look like? If you are summarizing income and expenses by the month, make two columns. The first column is for the names of the categories of both income and expenses, and the second column will hold the amounts budgeted for each item.

First, list your income and then list your expenses. The first two entries under income will be His Income and Her Income, and the next will be Child Support Income. If you are a blended family, you may be receiving some form of child support from his ex-wife or her ex-husband. Why would this be included in the family income? If the children are either his or hers, shouldn't that money be his or hers to spend as they wish? Sadly, this issue becomes a bone of contention in many blended families.

It is true that child support is for the support of the children, but if one spouse keeps it separate and lavishes it only upon their children, they take the risk of tearing the family apart. Some people would respectfully disagree, but personally I cannot see how a blended family can keep such monies separate. If all the money does not go into the same pot, then one or the other has access to money that their partner doesn't, and that won't work.

In the same way that child support may be an income item in your budget, it may also be an expense item. Many families send money elsewhere, to ex-spouses, to support their children.

Child support can be a hefty part of your budget, but it is a responsibility that you cannot afford to shirk. When our children were still small, I was paying $600 a month child support to their mother. It was a lot of money for that time, taking most of one paycheck sometimes.

Once the child support comes out of your income, you have other things to think about—the tithe, your savings, your vacation, your Christmas club, etc. Then there are the normal day-to-day expenses, and they must be listed by category: beauty supplies, haircuts, car insurance, car payments, car maintenance, groceries, gasoline, credit card payments…anything and everything you can think of. List it all down.

Next, add up all of the income, and add up all of the expenses, and then subtract the expenses from the income. The difference represents what is left over for discretionary spending.

Once you have your list of expenses done, you can begin to think about how your percentages compare with the average family. Experts tell us that 25 to 40 percent of your budget should go for housing. Twenty to 35 percent should go for food and other household expenses. Seven to 13 percent should go toward your car payment.

The very best way, of course, is not to have any car payment at all. Save your money until you can buy a car outright. It may not be the car you want, but at least it will be paid for.

Other expenses should be in the following range:

- 7% (no more than that) for consumer debt, paying off credit cards
- 6% to 10% for insurance
- 6% to 9% for entertainment, recreation, and vacation
- 5% to 7% for clothing
- 5% to 10% for savings
- 3% to 4% for gifts and Christmas
- 2% to 4% for allowances
- 2% to 8% for furniture
- 2% to 5% for education
- 5% for contingencies

Get everything into the mix. If, for example, you have a lawn service for your house, include that. The money to pay it will not magically appear. Determine ahead of time how much money will be needed.

Impulse Buying

Developing a budget is especially important for impulse buyers, and I am one of them. Impulse buyers go into a store, see something they like, and they want it right then. I have learned to carry around any item I pick up on impulse in a store for fifteen minutes before I go to the checkout counter. Often, I will lay it down in five or ten minutes after that initial rush of wanting it has passed. Usually, through this process, I come to my senses and am saved from myself before I get out of the store.

The problem is that when I do come to my senses and decide to leave something behind, I leave it right where I'm standing—not where I found it. For the people who stock the store, I must be their worst nightmare. I have left countless items scattered about all over the stores.

Another safeguard that we have put into place (because of my tendency to buy on sight) is that we never make a decision the same day on a large-ticket item. If you've ever gone to a time-share demonstration, you'll know why this drives those salesmen absolutely crazy.

We tell them up front that we never buy on the day we are presented to, and they say that this isn't a problem. But at the end of the presentation, the sales manager always gets called in to give us a final push to buy.

"We told you we would not buy today," we tell them with a smile. "We'll think about it overnight, and if we still want it tomorrow, we'll call you."

Of course their policy is that you can't buy it tomorrow. "Well, then if we can't buy it tomorrow, we don't want it," we answer.

"We'll give you one thousand dollars off the regular price if you buy today," the salesman insists.

"Well, if that's a legitimate offer, then you can give us a thousand dollars off tomorrow. And if you don't want to do that, then we don't want to buy."

Eventually we do escape unharmed, but we know that we've been through the combat zone.

When a vacuum sweeper salesman comes to our house, even if we have just vacuumed, he finds all kinds of dirt in our carpet. He shows it to us and insists that we need his machine, and I'm immediately convinced. On top of the amazing dirt demonstration, the man has made such an effort to present his product that it seems to me that we will be offending him if we don't buy. We just have to buy. That's all there is to it.

Again, I am saved only by our agreement never to buy the same day, and this goes for buying cars too. We need this safeguard because I am too easy to convince, and I need time to think over the consequences of a purchase.

What happens to millions of buyers like me is called "buyer's remorse." There's also a more technical term for it that some may recognize: cognitive dissonance.

Talking with a gifted salesman is a lot like standing in the reception line at a wedding: By the time hundreds of people have filed by and congratulated you on making such a good decision, you begin to believe that maybe it was a good decision after all. Impulse buyers need systems in place to protect them from themselves.

We have tried to teach these same principles to our children, especially to think about a purchase overnight, and if they still want it tomorrow, then to go buy it. When Sissy (Carrie) was still quite small, she wanted to buy a doll, but she was two dollars short. "Can I borrow two dollars?" she urged. "I want it so bad."

"You can work it off when we get home," we offered, and she agreed.

When we got home, we didn't forget, and Sissy was assigned to scrub the bathtub and the shower wall to work off her debt. She went in there and started the work, but before long she came out saying, "Whew! I wish I hadn't bought that dumb thing." It seemed to take her forever to get her assigned task done, and by the time she did, she was very sorry indeed that she had made the purchase. Many of us adults know just how she felt.

I have things that I haven't touched in years. When they were new, there seemed to be such joy just in owning them. But that joy quickly faded, and they no longer bring us pleasure.

Two Models of Budgeting

Lorrie and I had two models of finance management we could choose from: one from my parents and the other from hers. My parents never made provision for the future. After all, Jesus was coming soon, and any day now California would break off and fall into the ocean. So they made sure the banks they owed money to were located in California, and they believed that when the big drop-off came, they would not have to repay the money they owed. They wrote checks by faith when there was no money in the account, and if a check bounced, they were not embarrassed by it.

It was also possible to leave one town and go to the next, and because they didn't have computers in those days, creditors usually couldn't find you. In this way, my parents made their way through life, with absolutely no provision for the future.

When they reached retirement age, they lived in a small, cramped apartment that cost them fully half of their monthly Social Security check. And, from that point on until they died, life was harder for them than it should have been.

Lorrie's parents took a very different approach to finances. By the time they reached retirement, their home was paid for, and they had money saved to supplement their living expenses. They were not wealthy, but they were able to trade cars every few years, and they could take a trip when it suited them. Amazingly, my father-in-law was able to retire at the age of fifty-eight, when he and my mother-in-law still had many years left to enjoy life together.

These were the two models we had to consider. One of them seemed totally dysfunctional, and the other was well thought out and organized. It didn't seem like much of a choice. If you don't have a good model in your family to inspire you, look elsewhere.

The Ten Commandments of Budgeting

1. You shall not live above your means.

Invariably, when people ask for my help with budgeting, they never have enough money to make ends meet. There are always more expenses than income.

"Do you have cable television?" I ask.

"Yes."

"Well, you can't afford it," I tell them. "Have it cut off."

"I can't do that," they usually object.

"Oh, yes you can," I insist. "Install some rabbit ears so that you can get a few local stations. Then get rid of the cable. It's too costly."

"What sort of calling plan do you have on your telephone?" I ask them, and the answer is often that they have call forwarding, call waiting, caller ID, and a host of other services, and it's all costing them money.

"You can't afford all of that," I tell them. "Have it discontinued."

"What kind of car are you driving?" I ask. "How much is your car payment every month?" And they tell me.

"Sell it," is usually my necessary verdict, "and buy something that has a much lower monthly payment. If you can afford to buy a used car and pay cash, that's even better. Then you won't have any car payment at all. It may not look nearly as good, but at least you can go on living."

"Now, what about your housing expense? You can't afford $1,200 a month. You need to look for something that is more in the $800 a month range."

"I've thought about that," they reply, "and I just can't do it."

"Oh, but you can," I insist.

Why is it that we expect to live way above our means and then can't understand it when we are unable to meet our monthly obligations? You need to get rid of your pride, so that you can have financial breathing room.

"Oh, we could never go backwards," people tell me.

Why not? The kind of debt that people get themselves into by living above their means is terribly hard to recover from, and that's why personal bankruptcies are now at an all-time high.

If you are getting in over your head, you have to start cutting somewhere, or you'll eventually drown in debt.

2. You shall give of your abundance to God.

Hopefully, this is a principle we all agree on.

3. You shall save a portion of your income.

If you never save, you are eating your seed. Failure to save in the good times means that you will have nothing to live on when hard times come (and they do come). Crises of all sorts hit families when they least expect it. If you are spending everything that comes through your hands, you'll have nothing left to fall back on. Find ways to save.

4. You shall begin plans for retirement in your youth.

Now is the time to start—regardless of your present age. Make some saving plan—however small—and stick with it.

5. You shall share all financial burdens, successes, and planning with your spouse.

Talk over all money matters. Talk about it when there's enough, and talk about it when there isn't enough.

Talk about your desires for the next family vacation, for example. Can you afford it? Can you not afford it? What can you afford to do? And what can you not afford to do?

> *With everything you own, ask yourself the question: "If God were to require this of me, could I just hand it to Him and walk away?"*

One of the dangers is always that one or the other partner will say, "Let's do it—whether we can afford it or not." I was like that. If Lorrie wanted something, then I was determined to make it happen. I would figure out how to pay for it later. That's not the wise way to go.

If you can't afford something, one partner should speak up and say, "I'm sorry, but we can't afford this." That's fiscal integrity.

6. You shall not make idols of money and material possessions.

With everything you own, ask yourself the question: "If God were to require this of me, could I just hand it to Him and walk away?" If you could do that, then you have given God title to all that is yours. If you know that you could not do that, it means that you are still holding tight to material possessions.

The fact that you are willing to give a thing to God does not mean that He will necessarily take it. It only means that things have no hold over you. If He should require them for any reason and for any period of time, you would be willing to relinquish them.

7. You shall not be buried by excessive debt.

Debt can kill you quicker than anything else. It would be impossible to overemphasize this fact.

In the early years of our marriage, when we were still charging things on credit cards, it was a constant headache. If we got home from a trip and found that we had spent two thousand dollars, and we only had one thousand to pay toward it, that left us a thousand dollars deeper in debt. One day I said to Lorrie, "Maybe we should apply for an American Express card. That way we would be forced to pay it off when each month's bill comes due." At the time, American Express left a cardholder no other option.

That seemed to work for us. Now, after years of developing discipline and better planning, we don't have to worry about that. We use a card that gives us miles for our purchases, and we pay the account off every month when it's due. If we got into trouble again, we could revert back to a card that would force us to make the payment every month.

8. You shall not fall into the trap of labeling resources and possessions as "yours" and "mine."

In our marriage, nothing is "Lorrie's," and nothing is "mine" (except for our small allowances). It's not her car or my car. It's not her money or my money. It's "our" car, "our" house, and "our" money (our savings belong to both of us).

9. You shall allow resources for unexpected items.

After you have budgeted all of your expenses, you have to have something left over. You can't budget right to the penny. There will always be unforeseen expenses, and you will need a way to pay for them when they occur.

10. You shall direct and control your money rather than letting your money direct and control you.

Get out in front of your financial situation and tell your money where you want it to go rather than just simply tracking where it has all gone.

Warning Signals of Credit Problems

There are some warning signals that indicate that you are getting into credit problems. Put them in place and listen when the bells go off:

143

A. *Receiving calls or notices from creditors demanding payment.* If this happens, you're already in trouble.

B. *Paying only the minimum on credit balances.* If you pay only the minimum required on your credit card balances, you will probably not be able to pay off the principal in your lifetime.

C. *Using credit to pay for other credit purchases.* "We consolidated," is a common term being used these days, and those who do it believe that they now have a lot more money to work with. But this practice only leads to further indebtedness. A couple I once counseled was in deep financial trouble. She was involved in a serious automobile accident, and the resulting insurance settlement allowed them to pay off their entire indebtedness. But they didn't learn their lesson, and they didn't change their habits, so they got right back into financial difficulty. This time, they were able to slowly pull themselves out of the hole (five dollars at a time) and, more importantly, they changed so that this didn't happen to them again. Debt consolidation looks good on paper, but it usually only makes the debtors even more indebted and even more irresponsible. In the future, they may need to consolidate again and again...until they finally end up in bankruptcy.

D. *Using credit to buy basic necessities.* Never charge groceries or clothes or other necessities. Pay for them as you go.

E. *Spending more than 20 percent of your net income on debt reduction (paying off credit card purchases).* If more than 20 percent of your income is going to repay credit card debt, then you're in financial difficulty.

F. *Being unable to say exactly how much is owed on installment loans or long-term debt.* If you don't even know how much you owe, how can you ever repay it?

G. *Postponing payments due to lack of funds.* "I just can't make the payment this month," is a sad commentary. If it happens, recognize that you're in financial difficulty and do whatever is necessary to get your finances under control.

How to Go About Getting Out of Debt

Now that we recognize the problem, how do we solve it? How can we get out of debt?

Let's say that you owe $2,000 on one account, $1,000 on another, $500 on another, and $300 on another. Most people try to concentrate their available funds on the larger debt, but that's a mistake. Pay off the smaller debt first.

Let's say that you're paying $25 a month on that smallest account. When you have paid it off, don't feel that you now have an extra $25 a month that has suddenly been freed up to spend on other things. Concentrating on debt reduction and the benefits it will reap for the rest of your life, take that $25, add it to what you were already paying on the next smallest account (let's say $50), and start concentrating on paying that one off too.

When you insist on living on borrowed money, you are living above your means.

Once you have paid off that next account, you again have a choice to make. You could say that you now have $75 a month more available to you to spend each month, but that would be irresponsible. Debt reduction is the important matter at hand. Take that $75 a month, combine it with your already existing payment on the next largest account, and keep paying the additional amount on it ... until it, too, is paid off.

If you will not falter in your commitment, you can continue in this way until all of your debts are paid. The choice is yours. You can have a party and blow the additional amount, or you can invest it in the future of your marriage by paying down your common debt.

Unless you hit the lottery, this is the only way to effectively get out of debt. When you seem to have extra money, but you have existing debts, the truth is that you don't have any extra money. Put it where it will pay the greatest long-term dividends.

When you insist on living on borrowed money, you are living above your means. Let's take an example. If you borrow $4,800 and need to pay back $80 a month plus interest over the next five years, that means that you are living at least $80 a month over your income.

This is a conservative estimate. Most Americans are far deeper in debt than that. And, amazingly, many are borrowing at astronomical rates of interest. The interest rate on many credit cards is now at 14.9 percent, 18 percent, and sometimes even as much as 22 percent.

Let's say that you make only your minimum payment and you allow the interest on this loan to accrue. If you will look at an amortization schedule, a chart showing the breakdown of principal and interest for each payment, you'll see that you are sinking $960 more in debt each year. By the time five years rolls around, your debt will have risen to $8,104.

Now, when you see that, you start making more serious payments. If you pay $203 a month, the total of your payback will still be $12,190. And, remember, you only borrowed $4,800 in the first place.

When you started all of this, you were living $80 over your budget. Now, that $80 is gone, and you have lowered your standard of living by $203 a month. This is a sad commentary on the American financial system. Get free of it just as quickly as possible.

Budgeting When You Own Your Own Business

How can you budget when you operate your own business, and your income fluctuates from month to month? You will have to estimate how much you will earn from your business after expenses in a year, divide that by twelve, and then use that figure as your income. It will take time to know if that figure is a fair one, and you may later have to make some adjustments.

When I had a full-time counseling practice, I had good months and bad months. We decided that I would take out the same amount of money each month, regardless of how things were going. The first month I had was a good one, and the second was also good, and then I had a slow third month. But that month I wrote myself a check out of the business account for the very same amount, knowing that the good months and the bad months would eventually balance themselves out. Any surplus stayed in the business to take care of leaner times. Having this type of consistent income made it easier for us to budget our expenses.

If, after a year, there were still surplus funds in the business, then we could consider taking a special vacation, giving me a raise, or using more money for

Christmas. But we were careful never to take so much money out of the business that we placed it in financial jeopardy.

Those who don't adopt this or some similar system experience what is known as feast or famine. They have more than enough some months (and so they overspend), and they have much less than they need other months. This makes it very difficult to plan. Several good months in a row can give you a false feeling of security and cause you to spend way too much. An average over time is the only way to arrive at a reasonable and fair amount.

Give Each Other a Break

Early in our marriage I was not nearly as good about money matters as I became through the years. This troubled Lorrie and made her feel rather insecure. Would I be able to care for her as she needed me to?

Because of this, Lorrie labeled me as being fiscally irresponsible. I, in turn, put a label on her: controller. "It must be because you were the firstborn," I suggested. These, obviously, were not healthy views for us to hold of each other.

Over time, I became more and more disciplined about money matters, until I became quite possibly more conservative than she was in this regard. And she got over her controlling ways. Still, the labels stuck.

Fifteen years passed, and we received some money we had not budgeted. I suggested that we put it aside in a special account for a special purpose, and when we agreed on that plan of action, I set about to open the account and deposit the money. This troubled Lorrie. "But will the money be there when we get ready for it?" she said.

Those words stung. Year after year I had demonstrated solid fiscal integrity to her, and still she wanted to label me as fiscally irresponsible.

But, I realized, I sometimes did the same thing to her. When she made a comment about my driving, I would respond, "Oh, there goes the firstborn controller again." And Lorrie was definitely no longer a controller; she had given that up a long time ago. It was time that we let each other out of the box and stop placing undeserved labels on each other.

Start trusting each other in matters of money, and it will do wonders for your relationship. It's important to encourage each one and to forgive one another for past errors in money management. It was important that I forgive

Lorrie for having been controlling, and it was important that she forgive me for my fiscal irresponsibility. We had to put all that in the past and start afresh.

You can start a new chapter in your lives too, a chapter free of the constant recriminations often associated with money matters. To start, ask God to forgive you for mismanaging the resources He has placed within your hands. He gives us certain means, and it's up to us what we do with them. This is important because God will never give us more than we can manage effectively. The Bible says that if we are faithful over a few things, He will make us ruler over many things (see Matthew 25:21). This means that if we handle our money well, He will give us more.

When we don't seem to have enough money, it's not always the case that we have squandered what we did have. So, don't beat yourself up over this issue. But if you truly have not been a good steward, why would God want to give you more? If you have not learned to manage well what you already have, don't expect more.

Stand in front of a mirror and take a good look at your problem. It's you. Then let God change you and make you what He wants you to be. With that done, you and your mate can begin to find the true happiness and fulfillment God has destined for you and the financial prosperity promised by His Word.

The Issue of Control

(Or What God Thinks About Power Issues and Submission)

Submit to one another out of reverence for Christ. Ephesians 5:21

The whole issue of control that plagues so many marriages today is nothing new; it began a very long time ago in the Garden of Eden.

What Is Control? And Where Did It Originate?

Try to picture, if you can, what happened there in the garden and what the life of the first man and woman was like with God before the Fall. In Eden, everything was beautiful. The trees were lush and green, and the animals all walked about freely because there was no conflict.

Adam and Eve, too, were in perfect harmony with God, with each other, and with their natural surroundings, and there was no fear, no strife, no contention, and certainly no power struggle. Theirs was a perfect world ... that is until someone slithered in to spoil it all.

Satan has not changed. His purpose today, as it always has been, is *"to steal and kill and destroy"* (John 10:10). He is the author of the confusion that marred the perfection of Eden, and he is the author of the confusion that destroys many marriages today.

The chaos that followed Satan's intervention in the garden included a curse upon every man: that he would have to work very hard to earn enough to even survive (see Genesis 3:17-19). It also included a curse upon the woman:

I will greatly increase your pains in childbearing; with pain you will give birth to children. Your desire will be for your husband and he will rule over you. Genesis 3:16

For many years I thought that Adam must not have been present when Eve was tempted and succumbed; he surely must have been in some other part of the garden. Then I realized that Adam was actually right there by her side. But she had tasted sin, and he was still pure. It was the only time in history that two mortals faced each other—one of them sinless and the other a sinner.

I let my mind run free and began to wonder what manipulative strategies Eve had in her now sinful mind that she could use against Adam. What was it that she did to convince him to partake of her sin? Whatever it was, it worked. Adam, too, sinned.

Once Adam had also succumbed to sin, God pronounced the consequences over the both of them. Part of that consequence was His pronouncement over the woman: *"Your desire will be for your husband."*

It seemed strange to me that a woman's desire for her husband would somehow be considered a curse. I certainly want Lorrie to desire me, and I know she wants to desire me. And how could that be a curse?

The answer to this question came to me with the discovery a few chapters later in Genesis that the same Hebrew word translated as *desire* was used again (see Genesis 4:6). It says there that sin desired to take control of Cain, one of Adam's sons. If we were to apply this same principle to a woman's desire for her husband, it would mean that she was born with the desire to control him. This would not be unusual, for the desire to control is apparently a result of the Fall for both men and women.

We would never consider it to be a character flaw or a defect of personality for a woman to have pain in childbirth. So, why should we consider this part of the curse to be any different? This is just a fact of life that we all have to take into consideration.

Since the effects of the curse have fallen equally upon men and women, I believe in a balanced submission to one another through discipline. Bear with me as I lay out what I believe to be God's will for us today in marriage.

Most women seek to marry a strong man because they despise a man they can walk all over. They also don't want a man who always seeks to dominate them, abuse them, or refuse them equality in the marriage. They want a man who is their match, but who will lead them in a godly way.

Most women seek to marry a strong man because they despise a man they can walk all over.

Before sin, man and woman were mutually submissive, and there were no power issues. Neither was to be in charge of the other; neither was to rule over the other. There is nothing in the Bible to indicate anything other than an egalitarian relationship intended by God between man and God's gift to him—woman. But after sin, all loving submission ceased, and now we must submit to one another out of obedience.

When we do submit, it is in contradiction to what our flesh wants, because that's not how we're built. We submit because God has said that men are to be in submission to Christ as He is in submission to His Father, wives are to be in submission to their husbands, children are to be in submission to their parents, and all of us are to be in submission to our employers and our elders. We do this out of obedience.

But does it happen in most marriages? Not really. Submission is the ideal, and most marriages are far from ideal. Most of us still have many control issues that need to be dealt with.

Where did we learn these patterns of control? The first place we learned them, of course, was from example, from what was modeled before us as we grew up.

For instance, I am a lot like my father. Whenever I get really angry, my tendency is to withdraw. Often I go find something to do around the house, some housecleaning, for example. That's very similar to what he would do. He would get out his tool box and whistle to himself as he puttered around doing something with his tools.

The problem is that what we have learned from our parents often is not consistent with the teachings of the Word of God, and we need to make some changes. Also, we can become the recipients of generational curses inadvertently passed down from our parents and theirs.

Some of us have learned bad habits from our church leaders. One man said to me in the presence of his wife, "If she could just understand that I hear from God. The Holy Spirit shows me what to do, and if she would just do what I tell her, we could get along fine."

"I guess so," I answered. "Where can I sign up for that? It sounds wonderful." We have all heard submission taught from the pulpit in this way, as an absolute (women must obey without question all that their husband tells them), but in reality, it just doesn't work that way. Those who teach this are not obeying the scripture:

Do your best to present yourself to God as one approved, a workman who does not need to be ashamed and who correctly handles the word of truth.
2 Timothy 2:15

The world, on the other hand, is teaching a totally different viewpoint. Even our schools are presenting a completely egalitarian point of view, as taught by the women's liberation movement, that a woman must take control of every issue of her life. That also does not make for a healthy marriage relationship.

There is the world's view, there is your view, and there is God's view, and only His view will bring blessing. Adopting a distorted Christian viewpoint will do just as much damage as adopting a worldly viewpoint.

Traditional Views of Power

Studies have been done that reveal the traditional views of power. With agreeing or disagreeing, allow me to point out what some such studies have shown. [21]

On Financial Matters

Power struggles are most often played out in matters of finances. Studies have shown that dual-career couples engage in greater levels of power strategies than those in traditional marriages. If both are earning, then both feel like they have power in the relationship. The disparity comes in when one partner is earning and the other is not. The person earning (when the other is not) or the person earning most thinks they should have the most power. Of course, this is not right. Money should have nothing to do with who is in charge and who is not.

Traditionally, power in the family increases for women in proportion to the number of years they have worked outside the home—regardless of whether or not they continue to work after marriage. The more you've worked outside the home, ladies, the more you've learned that you don't have to put up with any nonsense from your spouse.

If men can isolate their wives, the issue of power becomes much more extreme. Wives, in this case, have only their husbands to trust, and they don't know any better. Dual-career couples never get into this type of power struggle because the women know too much.

Traditionally, on economic issues, the closer a wife's own tangible resources approximate those of her husband the more she can exercise bargaining rights to get him to share power. For instance, if a woman earns well, her husband is much more likely to help her with the cooking, the cleaning, and the laundry. It's not that he enjoys these chores any more than he normally would. It's just that the extra money coming in loosens up his willingness to sacrifice.

On Romantic Issues

On romantic issues, wives historically exert power over their husbands simply by manipulating a stronger flow of love from the husband than they reciprocate. If Lorrie could get me to desire her more than she desires me, think of the control she would have. Studies show that when spouses perceive themselves to be equally in love, marital power is shared equally.

Much of the romantic control women exercise over their men is sexual. They hold the trump card of sex and they can dangle it before their husband at any moment they feel it is needed. "If you want this, then you will do this."

In this way, women can keep their man dangling on a string like a puppet. In their hands, sex becomes like the carrot on a stick used to get the mule to do what he's supposed to do. And if he doesn't, he doesn't get the prize. It's as simple as that.

But sex is not the only tool women have at their disposal to exercise control over their husbands. They can also cut them off from friendship and emotional support.

Where issues of intimacy and sex are concerned, the balance of power always resides with the mate who has the most toys, who possesses the greatest number of the highly-prized possessions. Does she have more things that I want? Or do I have more things that she wants? These "things" might be any show of affection or concern, any granting of love, emotional or physical. Kissing, for instance, can be one of them. It is anything that we need from each other.

Interestingly enough, studies show that the power of the wife declines with the number of children born after the first one. The first child doesn't seem to affect the balance of power, but after that, the power of the woman declines because she is now perceived more as a mother than as an equal spouse, and she now has more children to attend to.

In the same measure, the husband's power reaches its peak just before the oldest child begins school. Once the children are in school, the mother begins to interact with other mothers, the teachers in the school, and others in the community, and some of the power she has lost is restored to her.

Again, I'm not saying that this is right. I'm just pointing out what studies have shown.

On Age Issues

Studies have shown that the relative power of the wife peaks at middle age, while the relative power of the husband does not peak until retirement because power is often associated with occupational status and income—what a person brings to the table. When that is lost, then their power begins to decline.

This is complicated by the fact that the home is often considered to be her territory. She has a long-established power base there. When a man begins to stay home more, his wife takes on a greater authority over him.

How We Control Each Other

So how do we control each other? There are some very subtle things that we use to accomplish it. Let us discuss some of them:

We Seek to Control Each Other with Anger

The one who gets angriest and shouts the most wins. We escalate the shouting, and we find ourselves on top…until someone else escalates it further. This goes on until suddenly we find ourselves tiptoeing around each other's anger.

If a mate is easily angered, then we cannot relate normally, and neither can the children. We all learn to tiptoe around the house so as not to disturb such a person and cause another outburst. This works so well that eventually just the threat of anger is enough to control us.

If you've ever lived around an angry person, you know exactly what I mean. The moment their anger begins to escalate, everyone in the house is looking for a way to appease them and to avoid further escalation of the matter. There are certain issues we learn to avoid, certain people we learn not to mention.

Controlling with anger is unacceptable in a marriage. As we have seen, the Bible says that we are to *"be quick to listen, slow to speak and slow to become angry"* (James 1:19). It also says, *"Be ye angry and sin not"* (Ephesians 4:26 KJV) or "In your anger do not sin." Anger is a healthy emotion, but it is never to be abused and allowed to hurt our spouse or our children.

We Seek to Control Each Other with Guilt

Guilt is a powerful controller. The accusation from a wife when she is chastising her husband might include words like these: "How do you call yourself a spiritual leader?" As Christians, we must never use the Bible and the elements of our faith in God to hammer one another. That's not their purpose.

One woman opened the Bible, pointed to First Corinthians 13, and said to her husband, "How can you call yourself a Christian and say you love me when you don't obey First Corinthians 13?" The man said it was the first time she had opened the Bible in a month. She just wanted to put him on a guilt trip.

God didn't call us to use His Word against each other, and doing so constitutes spiritual and biblical abuse. The only way you can effectively quote the Bible to each other is with a desire to build each other up. And more of us need to do that.

Christians, it seems, use the Bible only when it suits them and only to get their way. It's almost as if they are saying, "I want my way, and I can prove that it's best by the Scriptures."

When a couple comes into our counseling office, and one of them has a Bible in their hand, I sense trouble. I tell them, "Only one person is going to quote the Bible during this session, and that person is going to be me." I go on to explain my reasoning: "It is very probable that I am the only one here who is unbiased and will not use a biblical quotation as a weapon against one of you. Because I am neutral in this matter, I know that I can rightly divide the truth. Because you are both in a very emotional situation, you may not be able to remain as unbiased."

That doesn't mean that I never make a mistake in counseling, but if I do, it's at least an honest mistake, not based on a desire to beat someone up.

As a child, I often witnessed my parents whacking each other over the head with the Bible. Not literally, of course, but they were quoting it at each other constantly.

We Seek to Control Each Other with Money

In most every family, the one with the most money gets the most say—whether they are the most spiritual or not. "I'm the one working in this family, and I make the money, so what I say goes." This is so sad because it develops a top-down relationship in which there is never hope for equality.

The one making the money (or making the most money) actually takes on a parenting role and begins to treat even their spouse as a child. They become scolding and constantly offer lectures on what they perceive as proper behavior. God never intended for the husband/wife relationship to be one in which one mate spends their time scolding and lecturing the other.

Lorrie became a top flight manager, and sometimes when she came home, she forgot that she wasn't still at work with all the people she had to manage. Quietly and lovingly I would say to her, "I'm not your child, and I'm not your employee. Put that attitude away till tomorrow morning. You can go back to that when you get back to work."

We Seek to Control Each Other with Sex

It is very easy (and very common) to withhold sex as a means of getting the other partner to do what we want them to do. This is sad, because in this way, sex becomes a favor, not a sharing of mutual love. It is something to be bargained for, not something we willing and joyfully share. It is a reward or it is a punishment, and it should be neither of these.

We manipulate each other by threatening, either directly or indirectly, "I will allow you to be involved with me sexually if you do what I want, and I will withhold my sexual favors if you don't do what I want." This is a very powerful tool of control, and one that should never be used in a Christian relationship.

It is not right for a man to use this tool against his wife, and it is not right for a woman to use this tool against her husband. Sexual intimacy is something to be enjoyed between two loving people. It draws you together as equals, and is to be celebrated and enjoyed as such—not for the purpose of brokering power. We must never cheapen it by indicating that it is something being bought or traded. It must be willingly and lovingly given, or it is not the sex that God instituted.

We Seek to Control Each Other by Being Moody and Silent

This form of control, pouting, etc., is just as bad as any of the others, and we all know it only too well.

A friend I used to work with once told me this story when he came back from a weekend. He had been very excited when he left work on Friday evening because he and his wife were going on a long-anticipated skiing trip that Sunday. He woke up early Sunday and was anxious to get started, only to find that his wife seemed to have gotten up on the wrong side of the bed. She was all out of sorts. This made him angry, and the trip was off for the both of them.

When he told me the story, I said to him, "Why didn't you just go skiing without her? Why would you give her the power to spoil your day?" The next time it happened, he took my advice and went skiing anyway, and that seemed to turn things around for him.

Men do the same thing to their wives sometimes when they have something planned. Why is it that we delight in spoiling one another's fun, ruining one another's world. I'm afraid it's just because we know we can do it, and we use it as a form of punishment or coercion.

In my first marriage, my wife knew how to control me. She would suddenly and unexpectedly become ill. Anytime she didn't want to go somewhere with me, I could count on her getting sick at just the right moment. This happened especially if she knew that I was excited about going somewhere, and she wanted to punish me. What can you say when someone gets sick? You can't argue with that. It leaves you helpless and defenseless.

After I married Lorrie, the first time I wanted to do something and she got sick, I became very angry. It seemed like history was repeating itself all over again and that Lorrie, too, was trying to control me. It wasn't true, but it seemed to me to be true.

It happened again nearly twenty years later, and that old sick feeling came over my spirit again. We had paid several hundred dollars to attend a special Christmas function in another town, and I was looking forward to it, but that day Lorrie got sick.

She felt so bad about it that she got dressed and went with me anyway. But she really wasn't well, and when we arrived at the place, she was feeling so badly that she could hardly put one foot in front of the other.

We had taken a room in the Christian facility and were only three hundred yards from the event in question, but I didn't want to go alone. So I sat in the room fuming for a while. Eventually, I had to say to Lorrie, "This is not about you. It's about my 'stuff.' I'm angry because this is the way I was controlled in the past. You didn't do anything wrong. I'm sorry. I just need to work through this." I got in the car and went for a drive so that I could get hold of myself. The feelings of the past were just that terrible.

In many ways, what I was feeling didn't even make sense. I never suspected for a moment that Lorrie had done this thing on purpose. She would have loved to be there just as much as I, but still the experience upset me. Control is a terrible thing that sometimes leaves permanent scars upon our lives.

We Seek to Control Each Other with Threats of Leaving

"I'm leaving," my ex-wife often threatened.

"Please don't leave because I love you," I would plead, but in the process something would die a little within me.

"I'm leaving," she would threaten the next time.

"Please don't go; you're very special to me," I would answer, but again something within me died a little.

This went on until one day she said to me, "I'm going to leave," and I surprised even myself by answering, "That's fine; I no longer care." Something within me had completely died.

Later I learned that this had been nothing more than her way of asking me to affirm her. When she would threaten to leave, she was wanting to hear that I really did care and that I did not want her to go. But by the time I realized what was really happening, I was already dead inside. To me, it felt very much like an attempt at control, and this type of control is terrible.

> *The ultimate form of control is physical and often leads to charges of spousal abuse.*

We Seek to Control Each Other By Withholding Needs

Once we have confided in a mate what our greatest needs are, we have placed within their hands a most serious tool for controlling us. That's the risk we take. They know, better than anyone in the world, how to hurt us.

Such a tool should never ever be used against a mate, especially by one who calls themselves a Christian, but I am sad to say that it is often done nevertheless. Such an action is cruel, even vicious, and yet many are guilty of it—without seeming to realize how much harm they are doing.

We Seek to Control Each Other By Force

The ultimate form of control is physical and often leads to charges of spousal abuse. Put under the pressure of trying to get a mate to do what they don't want to do or to prevent them from doing something they do want to do, what we have come to call domestic violence often ensues.

A wife wants to leave the room, and her husband tries to keep her from leaving. She tries to run from him, and he grabs her and tries to hold her. She tries to drive away, and he beats on her windshield trying to prevent her from going, and it shatters.

People do strange things when they are desperate, when what is most important to them suddenly feels threatened. When every other form of control seems to be slipping away, if we're not careful, we will automatically resort to brute force. This is especially true of men, but domestic violence is not limited to men.

Whoever does it, control by force is totally inappropriate. It is never okay to resort to violence—whether you are a Christian or not. It is never appropriate to raise your hand against a mate. This includes shoving, restraining, holding, pushing, hitting, or throwing things at each other. This is totally inexcusable behavior, and it is not to be tolerated.

God doesn't condone such behavior in any way, shape, or fashion, and neither does society. Those who feel driven to such actions need to attend some anger management classes, and quickly.

The first time you use force in your relationship, you have breached an important wall and placed yourself in mortal danger. There's a break in the dam that must be repaired, and you can't just throw mud on it and hope that it will hold the next time a heavy rain comes along.

What Does the Bible Have to Say on This Subject of Control and Submission?

The Bible has a lot to say about this matter. Let us look at several passages briefly:

The Bible Teaches the Submission of Jesus to His Father

First, Jesus became our example and modeled submission for us. He said:

The one who sent me is with me; he has not left me alone, for I always do what pleases him. John 8:29

Christ was submitted to His Father, and we are to be submitted to Christ.

The Bible Also Teaches Us Submission to One Another

Submit to one another out of reverence for Christ. Ephesians 5:21

Submitting to each other in the marriage doesn't mean I'm always in charge, and it doesn't mean that Lorrie always has to do what I want to do.

Submitting to each other means that sometimes I do things for her, giving in to her, and sometimes she does things for me, giving in to me. In this way, the needs, and also the desires and expectations, of both can be met. Mutual submission also provides us a measure of security.

A couple who were on the verge of divorce came to me for last-minute counseling. The straw that seemed to have broken the camel's back was the fact that he was an accountant and thus should have known better, but he got them into some sort of speculative land deal, and they were now unable to make their payments and were about to lose everything. She blamed him for all of this, because he was the one who suggested that they take the deal.

But she had also signed the necessary papers. "Did anyone have a gun to your head when you signed?" I asked.

"No," she admitted.

"Did you sign that contract of your own free will?" I asked.

"Yes," she admitted.

"Did the two of you talk the matter over and decide it was what you wanted to do?" I asked.

"Yes," she admitted.

"Then why is it all *his* fault?" I asked.

That seemed to break the impasse. Once they could own the problem together, she could no longer use it as a means of controlling him.

In that moment, this couple had submitted to each other, and when we submit to each other, there is a joint responsibility for what happens. Consequently, we can no longer blame the other for the outcome. I cannot blame you, and you cannot blame me. Instead, we take joint responsibility for what happens. This frees us from control.

The Bible Teaches Submission of Wives to Their Husbands

Now we're getting into a very touchy area, and I want to be careful to rightly divide the Word of truth here. The Bible does say:

> *Wives, submit to your husbands as to the Lord. For the husband is the head of the wife as Christ is the head of the church, his body, of which he*

is the Savior. Now as the church submits to Christ, so also wives should submit to their husbands in everything. Ephesians 5:22-24

Does this mean that women must lie down and become doormats for their husbands? Of course not. In fact, it is interesting just what else the Scriptures have to say about this subject of wives being in submission to their husbands:

Wives, in the same way be submissive to your husbands so that, if any of them do not believe the word, they may be won over without words by the behavior of their wives, when they see the purity and reverence of your lives. 1 Peter 3:1-2

The wording of the *King James Version* is interesting here:

Likewise, ye wives, be in subjection to your own husbands; that, if any obey not the word, they also may without the word be won by the conversation of the wives; while they behold your chaste conversation coupled with fear. 1 Peter 3:1-2 KJV

The key is: *"while they behold."* There has to be something that they behold. Women, if you want to change your husband, you can do it *"without words."* He might rebel if you try to do it with words, but when you live out your faith before him, it is difficult for him to resist.

For Lorrie, there was a time in midlife when she bought into the concept of power as the world sees it. Later, she was to learn that there was a very big difference between what God perceived as power and what the world perceived as power.

She was working in the corporate world then, and in that atmosphere, she began to experience the pressure to have more equality, be in charge, and exercise more influence. She would need to do all of this if she expected to climb the corporate ladder, but it also began to spill over into our relationship.

When she began to see clearly what the Word of God had to say on this subject, she realized, she said, that she was totally out of order with regard to the family. Although I had never said a word to her about this, I had been praying that God would show us both what our proper roles were in the family. Just as she had been praying Psalm 1 over me, I had been praying Proverbs 31:10-31, The Wife of Noble Character, over her.

Her own prayer now became desperate and simple, "God, help me to be the wife You called me to be."

"If You will help me to do this thing," she prayed, "I'll do it. But You will have to show me how, for I have no idea how to do it myself."

Soon afterward she got hold of a book by Bunny Wilson called *Liberated Through Submission.*[22] That sounded like an oxymoron to her, but she soon discovered that there was real freedom to be found in doing things God's way. Through that book, she became convinced that her unwillingness to submit to me as her husband had hindered the freedom of God's hand in blessing our lives with everything He wanted to do for us.

God had called her to submission, and sometimes that meant that I would make a decision she didn't like, and she would be severely tested. When it happened, she would have to look into her heart to see what her motive was and to see if her attitude was right before God. If the motive was right and the attitude was right and she still didn't agree with me, she would have to pray and give it to God, she decided, for she no longer wanted to impede His blessings upon our lives.

After that day, when Lorrie first repented and turned her face toward God and His will for our lives, fully committing herself never to resist what He was doing in us, He began to teach her how to be submissive to me and to love every minute of it. It was exciting to her to be watching God at work as she did her part, and He did what He had promised.

She had worried needlessly about things she had no business worrying about, and now God was in control. If my heart needed to be changed, God would change it. She had tried to do it in the past, and in the process had tried to control and manipulate me and place herself in charge—just as the world had taught her she needed to do.

She had done that well, but now she knew that she had been out of order, and she knew that God was at work for her. She wondered if other people had been praying for her along these same lines. Someone had been praying for her, because she was quickly becoming a woman after God's own heart.

Lorrie was deeply touched by the truth John the Revelator received directly from our Lord Jesus:

Behold, I am coming soon! My reward is with me, and I will give to everyone according to what he has done. Revelation 22:12

When each of us stands before God, a mate will not be there for us to blame, nor can they be an advocate for us in that moment. You and I will be held totally accountable for our actions when we eventually stand before the Almighty. Therefore it behooves each of us to follow God's plan with a proper attitude and a loving heart because we want to hear our Lord say to us one day:

Well done, good and faithful servant! Matthew 25:23

God Says to Men...

God has not left us men out when it comes to responsibility. In fact, ours is the dominant responsibility in the marriage and in the larger family. Therefore we urgently need to hear what God has to say to us.

Our wives are praying for us to change, but sometimes our pride won't permit it. If we want God's favor, we must choose to set aside our pride so that He can accomplish in us what He desires. The Scriptures say to us:

Husbands, in the same way be considerate as you live with your wives, and treat them with respect as the weaker partner and as heirs with you of the gracious gift of life, so that nothing will hinder your prayers. 1 Peter 3:7

This does not mean that women are innately weak, that they're inferior, or that they're anything less than we are. We are called to walk side by side with them as equals.

My wife was not called to stay under my feet, but she *is* to remain under my arm of protection. This is not because she is inferior, but because God has chosen to give me this responsibility.

In response, we husbands are to respect and love our wives *"as heirs with [us] of the gracious gift of life, so that nothing will hinder [our] prayers."* If your prayers are not being answered, men, take stock of the way you are treating your wife. Are you considerate of her? Are you loving enough to her?

Husbands, love your wives, just as Christ loved the church and gave him-self up for her... . Ephesians 5:25

This is a very critical piece of the puzzle, and we must be obedient to it. It all begins with *us*, not with our wives. It begins when *we* submit to Christ as He submitted to His heavenly Father. Ours is the first and greatest responsibility.

We are to love our wives as Christ loved the Church. What a great and holy commission! If I love Lorrie in that way, do you think she will have any trouble submitting herself to me?

There is no "if" in this passage, no condition that our wives must meet. Our responsibility stands—regardless of what our wives do.

We must answer to God first, and if we are doing our part, if we are loving our wives as Christ loved the Church, I can't believe that there is a woman alive who would not want to submit to that. Women are just waiting for the loving embrace of a true gentleman.

This is not the concept we men usually have of submission. Our concept is one in which we can dominate, and that's what we want to do. We want to be powerful and to demonstrate our power.

Over and over, in my counseling office, I hear men complaining, "My wife just doesn't understand submission," or "My wife doesn't understand that she is to be in submission to me. I made a decision, and she had the nerve to question me."

Well, she has that right. As men of the family, we must come to a conclusion about what we're going to do as a couple or as a family, but we may well be questioned. The problem may be more in how we're questioned (or perhaps challenged), rather than the fact that we are questioned or challenged.

For my part, I would not want to have full dictatorial powers over my home. That's more authority than I want or would know what to do with. If that were the case, then I alone would be responsible, and I would rather share responsibility. When the chips are down and a decision must be made, then I'll step up and make it—even if I don't want to. But I can do that only after Lorrie and I have talked everything over, and I am able to weigh her opinion and her thoughts on the subject. Giving up my pride, I can then make a sensible decision.

Submission Must Be Done Cheerfully

Submission on the wife's part isn't really submission until it can be done with a cheerful heart. One day Lorrie and I were driving in the mountains, and she said to me, "God's really been working in my life, and I think I'm doing pretty well on this issue of submission."

Submission does not mean that wives are doormats and that their husbands can walk all over them.

≈

I smiled and said, "You're doing great, but sometimes without much joy." Submission isn't complete until we can be cheerful and light about our obedience to the Word of God.

Some women say, "Okay, I'll submit, but you're in for it." "I'll submit, but I'll never let you forget it. And the next time an issue comes up, don't you dare forget what happened here." That's not true submission.

In the same way, we must all submit to God with a cheerful heart. When God requires something of us, we sometimes say, "Okay, whatever You want," but we do it grudgingly. It is when we follow His Word with a glad heart, knowing that His will is always best, that the blessing comes.

What Submission Is Not

Submission does not mean that wives are doormats and that their husbands can walk all over them. It does not mean that he is the family dictator. It does not mean that he has absolute control and authority over her. That would be abusive—any way you look at it.

Men are notorious for being controlling of their women. Given the opportunity, they will sometimes cut a woman off from friends and family. Then, when he abuses her, she has no one to turn to. If this is allowed to continue, the woman's self-esteem will be so diminished that she won't remember that she has any worth at all. At some point, she may even begin to believe this tortured woman is who she really is, and that's not right.

Ladies, submission does not mean that you are inferior. God created us, man and woman, to walk side-by-side as equals. God looked down on my ancestor Adam and said, "It's not good for you to be alone. I'll make a help-mate, a companion, a completer for you." And then God created Lorrie, and she is that completer for me.

Lorrie is not my servant. She is not at my side to do everything I tell her to do. She is not there so that I can have someone to abuse and put down. Putting a wife down makes some men feel bigger, but God has called us to walk side-by-side as heirs and joint heirs in all that He has destined us to do.

Yes, men, we do have to step out and take the lead. Of course we have to. That's our job. We didn't ask for it, but it has been given to us by God. But that doesn't mean that we leave her behind or that we put her down in order to get out in front. We walk side-by-side every step of the way, although we men are assigned to decide the particular direction of our steps.

Ladies, this doesn't mean that you will never participate in the decision-making of the home. Of course you will. Anytime there is a decision to be made, we cannot just announce our decisions and expect you to follow them. We talk them over together, and then we work them out together.

I don't just come home from work one day to do as some professing Christian men:

"This is what we're doing."

"I don't want to do that."

"You just shut up. That's what I said, and that's what we're doing. The Bible says that you have to be submissive to me, so let that be the end of it."

I know this happens, but it's never God's will. That's not what He has called us to, men. If we love our wives as Christ loved the Church, we will never act like that. Christ never behaved that way with His Church, and we cannot afford to do it with our wives.

Submission, especially in the present world climate, is not easy. Lorrie has to admit that it took her many years to get it right. Eventually she was able to say to me (after we had discussed something and were unable to reach a consensus), "Okay, Sweetheart, you have my opinion. Now, it's up to you to pray and make a final decision."

This works well for her, and other women might want to try it too. Have a healthy discussion, but when it's finished, back off, ladies, and pray for your husband that he will make the right decision.

When you do this, whatever your husband decides you will be blessed. If, on the other hand, you constantly oppose him, whatever he decides, you will be cursed. So the blessing or the cursing is more in your attitude of trust and obedience to God than in a perfect decision as you might envision it.

You do want your husband to make the very best decisions, so you will pray for him to do that, but be sure that you are not a hindrance to his decisions, rather than the helper he so desperately needs you to be.

Men, don't be afraid of the fact that you cannot take control until your wife gives you that right. That's how God has planned it. So the two of you must decide together.

Having differing viewpoints is not a bad thing. It is actually healthy because it prevents you from making hasty decisions. Since our wives often see things from a very different perspective, we must weigh that perspective before any decision is taken. Then, when she has given us the right to make the final decision, it's our responsibility to seek God and come up with an answer that will bless all concerned.

I know that it sounds easier than it really is. Each of us has a strong opinion, and each of us feels that we are right. And who *is* right? Sometimes the man is right, and sometimes the woman is right. What is sure is that God always knows what is right, and if we choose to seek Him, He will guide our paths.

The man is never always right, and the woman is never always right, but God *is* always right. The man of the family is charged with seeking to know what God's best is for the entire family. This does not mean that the word of a husband or father is necessarily a command to the rest of the family. Because he is not the family dictator, he welcomes the opinions of others. In fact, he treasures their opinions, and He is respectful of their opinions. In the end, because he is charged with deciding what the right course is, he must defer to God's opinion.

Don't get so involved in giving your opinion that you cannot pause long enough to hear what God is saying. Since he is the Head of our household and the Master of our lives, we must let Him have His way. Earthly fathers may not always know best, but our heavenly Father always does.

So, does the husband always win and the wife always lose? Not at all. We're in this thing together. We have a mutual interest in all of this. Both will profit by a good decision and both will suffer from a bad one.

Women are not consigned to a life of slavery—not in any sense of the word. Women are not doomed to obey every whim of their husbands—not in any sense of the word. This is a walk that you take together before the Lord.

Submission doesn't mean that the man is the captain and the woman is the private, and she has to stand at attention and salute him when he comes in the door. In fact, it helps if the two are of equal rank. So try to advance together as much as possible, knowing that you are equals in God's sight.

Practical Approaches to Submission

So what can we do to deal with this power thing in the family in a practical way? Here are some ways that we can put the teachings of God's Word on this subject into practice:

1. Mutually determine who is in control of which parts of your lives and stick with that decision.

The real problem in marriage comes when there are two controllers married to each other. An instrument has been developed that can determine your nature and whether you like to control or to be controlled. When I give a couple this instrument and the results show that both parties have a need to control, I know that their case is particularly difficult. Whatever the profile shows, we need to divide power between us.

In our case, Lorrie's in charge (by mutual agreement) of certain parts of our lives, and I'm in change of others. She has full control over the areas she's in charge of, and vice versa. This does not mean that we don't seek the input of our mates in these areas. We do. But then we take full responsibility for the outcome.

Why would I, as a husband, relinquish control of anything? One, because it's too much for me to try to control absolutely everything. Two, if I fail to utilize Lorrie's assets, what kind of spiritual leader would I be? Lorrie is decidedly better than me in some areas, and if she's better, then she needs to be taking charge of that particular area. In this way, we try to find our areas of strength. If I had those resources at my fingertips and did nothing to put them to work, I would not be a very good manager.

If one partner is not very organized and the other is, obviously there are areas where the organized mate must be in charge—be it husband or wife. If one is a better money manager than the other, it would be absurd not to give that person change over the finances—be it husband or wife. If one partner is better at making social arrangements, why would we not want that person to be in change of this important area of life?

2. Accept the biblical pattern when you are polarized and allow for no compromises to be worked out.

The biblical pattern, again, is for the wife to say, "I don't agree with his viewpoint, but I will give him the right to seek God for the right decision, and I will pray for him to do what is best for us all." It is for the husband to say, "We can't seem to agree on this issue, and so I have an obligation to step out and make a final decision, taking into consideration her feelings on the matter."

3. Recognize when manipulation occurs by the use of power controllers.

Learn to recognize the means of control and refuse to accommodate them—either in yourself or your mate. When you find yourself trying to control a situation, repent, back up, and start over.

The Bible reveals that God knows every thought we have (see Hebrews 4:12). He knows our hearts, and He knows our every motive. When manipulation occurs, whether by male or female, somehow I think that we also know it deep inside. Other parties may not recognize it, but we do.

We can also ask God to help us recognize this by red flagging it for us when it happens. The Holy Spirit can convict our hearts and show us that our motives are not pure. Then, when you feel a check in your spirit, you will know to look again. Are you thinking thoughts that you shouldn't be thinking? Are you subconsciously trying to control your mate? Stop and start over.

4. Abandon modeled and learned behaviors and learn new behaviors for yourself.

We each have a rule book. I envision yours perched on your shoulder. You can easily flip the pages of it, so you know how to do everything because you have this rule book that tells you. With the help of family, friends, and associates, you have written everything that is in your rule book, and that is what guides your daily life.

The problem is that your rule book may or may not agree with the teachings of the Word of God. The behaviors in there are modeled behaviors and learned behaviors that have attached themselves to you over the years of your life. What you may have to do now is to actually tear out many of the existing pages of the rule book and rewrite them based on what you learn from God's Word. When this is done, you will have a new way of controlling behavior that is consistent with God's will and plan.

5. Be honest in the communication of your power needs.

Talk about what you need from your mate in this regard. How do you need them to relate to you? Work these things out together.

Lorrie has said that when she realized she was trying to control a given situation, she found that fear and insecurity were present in her heart. Since she was able to recognize this fact, she could overcome it. At times she had to admit to me what she was feeling and ask me to pray for her.

We make sure that we have a safe place where either of us can talk about anything at all, and neither she nor I make the other feel less of a person because they are feeling something deep inside. We may not always be able to resolve it at the moment the conflict arises, but after a time of examination, we usually come to a healthy conclusion.

6. Carefully consider the position of your spouse when deciding issues of control.

What is their need? What is their opinion? Talk it back and forth. Such conversations may be rather emotionally charged, and one or both of you may become quite animated. Move from one level of communication to the next until you can uncover the real need and address it.

7. When in conflict, refuse to let the issues of power prohibit you from seeking a compromise.

You don't have to win. The goal of conflict resolution is not to win, but to resolve the conflict. Don't allow your stubbornness, your need to control, your need to be in a position of power to keep you from reaching an acceptable compromise.

8. Don't make the mistake of seeking power and control in a relationship just because you feel unimportant and unfulfilled.

If I put you down, that doesn't make me look better. Sometimes our egos seem to get a boost because we are in control of our household. "I'm the man of the house, and I'm in charge here." This may fuel an ego, but it will do little else. Men, just because you're in charge doesn't make you "the big bad man."

Ladies, you are just as guilty sometimes. You're also not "the big bad woman" just because you feel the need to be in charge, and to do that you have to put your mate down.

9. Don't make unreasonable demands just to assert your control.

Never tell other people to do something, like give up a friend, just to test their love. There may be times, early in your relationship, when you will have to restrict some friendships, but this is the exception.

Lorrie and I did some things early in our relationship that paid long-term dividends. I told her about some people I felt threatened by, and she honored my feelings. One case in particular involved a business trip she was called on to take to California with a male associate. I shouldn't have been jealous, but I was, and I asked her not to meet him in social settings. It would have been quite normal for her to have dinner with him each evening so that they could plan their strategies for the next day, but she honored my feelings and excused herself five nights in a row.

For the first three years of our marriage, we agreed not to have lunch with a person of the opposite sex without first calling our mate and asking if it was acceptable. If I was invited to lunch, for instance, by one of my longtime secretaries, and Lorrie was not available to give me her consent, I just said something like "I'm not very hungry today. Thanks anyway."

For years, I had a faithful lady associate who had come up through the ranks with me. She was young enough to be my daughter, but the closeness of our work together bothered Lorrie, so (as difficult as it was logistically) I backed off from that relationship. The important thing was that we always asked the other how they felt about it, and we honored those feelings.

My ex-wife lived in Pueblo, and I worked in Pueblo, and sometimes she would call me at work to talk over something about the children. This bothered Lorrie, and she asked me not to take the calls at work, to wait until I was home, so that she could overhear the conversation and be satisfied in her heart that it was all business. The next time my ex-wife called, I told her that I wasn't able to talk right then, to please call me at home. That resolved the issue.

For years now, neither of us has felt threatened by someone else. If I did feel threatened again, I would not ask Lorrie to give up a friendship just to prove that I was in charge in our home. Instead, I would say to her, "That person being around you so closely makes me feel very uneasy. Would you mind not being so close to them until I feel a little better about it?" I have no doubt that Lorrie would willingly comply with any such sentiment expressed on my part, and she knows that I would do the same for her. We have nothing to test, nothing to prove, and no reason to make a power issue of this matter.

In the course of our work, Lorrie talks to many people, and I talk to many people, and we feel completely comfortable with this fact. Our mutual trust has given us great freedom. If any issue of insecurity arose with either of us, we both know that just a word would be all that was necessary to resolve it. Rather than deal with this as an issue of control, we deal with it as a matter of mutually meeting each other's needs.

10. Do not belittle your spouse in front of others just so that you can look important and in charge.

If you want to look like the worst idiot who ever lived, put your spouse down in public. This will assure you of the prize. Letting others know that your spouse is your lover and the number one person in your life does not diminish your importance in any way. To the contrary, choosing her as your life's mate and then turning on her and belittling her in public makes you look like an absolute fool. Why on earth would we ever imagine that doing something like this might make us look good?

11. Don't let the quest to be powerful drive you to actions that cause you to be feared.

Respect and fear may seem to be the same thing, but they're definitely not. What you are seeing in someone's eyes may not be respect at all, but fear. If you see fear in your children's eyes, you're in trouble as a father. If you see fear in your wife's eyes, you'd better go back to the drawing board. Something is very wrong with your relationship.

Our greatest challenge in submission is patience.

≋

Nothing in the Word of God teaches us that inspiring fear is good or acceptable. God has called you to deal with each other in a way that inspires respect and mutual admiration, not fear.

If you scream at a child and grab them violently, you will see terror in their eyes, and that is totally out of line. Learn to deal with your children without inspiring fear in their hearts.

Our Greatest Challenge in Submission

Our greatest challenge in submission is patience. The moment we submit to God, we expect Him to do everything He has promised, but He does things in His own time.

As Lorrie began submitting to me, I felt very uncomfortable about it. For one thing, I wasn't used to it, and for another, it forced me to take on responsibilities that I was not accustomed to. As she began to do what God had called her to do, it forced me to do what God had called me to do. Her stepping back created a void that I had to step into.

God began to move me into places I wasn't sure I ever wanted to go. But I had no choice. That's what !eadership is all about. I hadn't chosen to be there, but I was, so I had to make the best of it.

If I had tried to step into that place by force, rather than allowing God to put me there, I would have only set back His plan for us and, with it, His provision for us. It had to come in His time and in His way.

Submission, like love, is an act of our will, and it is only for those who desire to be totally obedient to God. In the Garden before the Fall, it was the natural way of things, but today it is contrary to the way of the world we learn from those around us and contrary to our sinful nature.

Because submission is an act of obedience, Ladies, you have a responsibility not to develop a passive-aggressive nature. Many women with strong husbands are

174

guilty of this sin. On the surface they seem to agree with their husband's leadership, but underneath, under the surface, there is a boiling cauldron waiting to erupt. Those who are passive-aggressive seek to undermine authority, and they do it with the use of subtle controllers.

Sometimes when a wife is overbearing, her husband becomes passive-aggressive. On the surface he seems to have given over control of the marriage to his wife, but under the surface he seeks to control her with moods, illnesses, silences, and other covert means. Men, don't you be guilty of this. God has not given you permission to recant your responsibilities. If your wife is overbearing, let God deal with her. You can't do it. All of your quoting of the Bible to her will not change her. Only God can do that, and He doesn't need your help.

Wives, you may feel that your husband is the problem, and if he would just change, everything would be all right. But you can't change him, only God can. So give the matter to God, and concentrate on yourself. You can't change your husband, and your husband can't change you. Only you can change you.

I have all I can handle to bring about the needed changes in my own life without trying to change Lorrie, and she has all she can handle to change herself without trying to change me. We must concentrate on our own needs and let God change the other person.

Early in our quest for God's will in our lives, Lorrie prayed earnestly for God to change me. Then God convicted her that she needed to concentrate on herself and convinced her that she could not change me. She knew that she was not yet the person God wanted her to be, so she needed to concentrate on her own areas of need and let God deal with me. From that day on, she dedicated herself to lifting me up and praying for me, and otherwise admiring and respecting me as God had commanded her to. With her obedience, the blessing would come. In the meantime, she would be patient and persevere. Let God change your heart, and He will take care of the rest.

Never Use the Submission Issue As a Substitute for Developing Good Conflict Resolution Skills

Those who use the issue of submission as a substitute for developing good conflict resolution skills have abused the Bible and failed in the responsibility left to them. Sometimes, men, when we don't know how to work out an issue, we try demanding that everyone obey us instead. That won't work because it's not

God's way. He has not established scriptural submission as a means for us to hammer our wives. Submission must be a blessing, or it is counterproductive.

Once, when I was teaching a class for premarital counseling, a man raised his hand and asked, "Would you explain what the Bible has to say about submission?"

"Why are you asking?" I countered. My fear was that, as men do, he wanted his fiancé, who was sitting next to him, to hear about submission in his presence so that he could later call her on it. I was willing to explain to her in private what the Bible said about submission, but I wasn't willing to give him ammunition to use against her. The Bible is more for living and less for lecturing one another.

Men, read well the portions of scripture that show us to be mutually submissive to each other, and let God deal with your wife about the rest. Concentrate on your need to love your wife as Christ loved the Church, and the rest will come. Learn how to obey the admonition, *"Be considerate...and treat them with respect...so that nothing will hinder your prayers"* (1 Peter 3:7), and leave the rest to God.

You read and study the portions of the Bible that directly relate to you, and let your wife read and study for herself the portions that directly relate to her. You cannot live her life for her, and she cannot live your life for you, and each of you must one day answer to God for your own actions.

The wonderful thing about the book *Liberated Through Submission* by Bunny Wilson is that it was written by a woman, from a woman's perspective.[23] That is as it should be.

Let God teach you to know His heart concerning the power struggles we all face in life and how power must be brokered in the marriage according to His Word, and you will be blessed.

Before Love Dies

(Or Keeping Courtship Alive)

My lover is mine and I am his.... Song of Solomon 2:16

What does a woman want in her man? At the age of twenty-two, one woman made the following list:

- *Handsome*
- *Charming*
- *Financially successful*
- *A caring listener*
- *Witty*

- *In good shape*
- *Dresses with style*
- *Appreciates the finer things*
- *Full of thoughtful surprises*
- *An imaginative, romantic lover*

Ten years later, at the age of thirty-two, she revised the list somewhat. Apparently her own tastes had changed a little, and her expectations had changed a lot:

- *Nice looking*
- *Preferably with hair on his head*
- *Opens car doors*

- *Holds chairs*
- *Has enough money for a nice dinner at a restaurant*

- *Listens more than he talks*
- *Laughs at my jokes at appropriate times*
- *Can carry in all the groceries with ease*
- *Owns at least one tie*
- *Appreciates a good home-cooked meal*
- *Remembers birthdays and anniversaries*
- *Seeks romance at least once a week*

By age forty-two, she had revised her list even more, as her expectations continued to decline:

- *Not too ugly*
- *Bald head's okay*
- *Doesn't drive off till I'm in the car*
- *Works steady*
- *Splurges on dinner at McDonalds sometimes*
- *Nods head at appropriate times when I'm talking*
- *Usually remembers the punch lines of jokes*
- *Is in good enough shape to rearrange the furniture*
- *Usually wears shirts that cover his stomach*
- *Knows not to buy champagne with screw-top lids*
- *Remembers to put the toilet seat down*
- *Shaves on most weekends*

By the time she had reached fifty-two, the list was again revised:

- *Keeps hair in nose and ears trimmed to appropriate length*
- *Doesn't belch or scratch in public*
- *Doesn't borrow money too often*
- *Doesn't nod off to sleep while I am emoting*
- *Doesn't retell the same jokes too many times*
- *Is in good enough shape to get off the couch on weekdays*
- *Usually wears matching socks and fresh underwear*

- *Appreciates a good TV dinner*
- *Remembers your name on occasion*
- *Shaves on some weekends*
- *Wears tennis shoes with suits*

Ten years later, the list had changed again to reflect her consistently lowering expectations:

- *Doesn't frighten small children*
- *Remembers where the bathroom is*
- *Doesn't require much money for upkeep*
- *Only snores lightly when awake*
- *Doesn't forget why he's laughing*
- *Is in good enough shape to stand up by himself*
- *Usually wears some clothes*
- *Likes soft foods*
- *Remembers where he left his teeth*

By the time the woman was seventy-two, she was just happy to have a man who could still breathe.

Nothing is more important than keeping romance alive in our relationships. It's what made the marriage work in the first place, and it's what will make the marriage work still. Why is it that romance seems to wane with time? We must not allow it to happen.

As we saw in Chapter Two, Scott Peck, in his book *The Road Less Traveled*,[24] has said that love is the discipline to continue doing in marriage what you did out of passion in courtship. It happened then out of passion, and it must be continued now out of loving discipline. In this chapter, let us examine seriously this all-important subject.

Why Does Romance Wane?

Why is it that so many couples stop being romantic after they get married? One answer may be that they have had wrong models to learn from, and consequently they don't know what real romance should look like.

This also explains why husbands and wives go into a marriage with far different expectations. One couple woke up the morning after returning from their honeymoon, and he lay there angry in bed because she wasn't getting up to prepare his breakfast (as his mother always had for his father), and she lay there angry in bed because he wasn't getting up to prepare her breakfast (as her father had for her mother). The two of them clearly had very different expectations, forged through childhood models, and neither of them had communicated well with their partner. This is a very common problem in marriage.

One reason that men stop being romantic is that they have already conquered their mate, and they thought romance was only for that purpose. As I noted in Chapter Two, they are now home from the hunt, and they have the prey all shot and bagged, and slung over their shoulder. So, to their way of thinking, it's over. They no longer have a need for romance.

Or so they think. What a mistake this is!

Another reason that is often cited for failing to keep romance alive in the marriage is the hectic pace of life. People get so busy doing all the things that have to be done that they don't have time to be romantic.

Another major reason cited for failing to keep romance alive is the coming of the children. "What would the children think if they saw us acting romantic?" they ask themselves. So they don't do it anymore.

With most people, romantic love just seems to wear off. This happens even with couples who vow that it never will. At the beginning, they are looking into each other's eyes, they can't keep their hands off of each other, they talk to each other all the time, and they seem to understand everything the other one is saying. Then, somehow, that all changes.

Is this just imagination? No. There is a scientific explanation to all of this. There are chemical reactions in our bodies that make us act the way we do, and the absence of those chemicals can make us change the way we act.

Back in the 1960s one of the popular drugs that was in use by the young people was known as PCP. This drug gave the user an intense high in which colors looked more vivid and sounds and emotions were amplified. Those who experienced it never forgot its effect. Now scientists have discovered that our bodies produce a chemical very similar to PCP when we are impassioned. That explains a lot, doesn't it.

When Lorrie and I were dating, I was living in Pueblo, Colorado, and she was living in Colorado Springs. One night we had talked on the telephone for several hours already, and it was past one o'clock in the morning when she said, "I would love to have some ice cream about now."

I got dressed and went out in search of a place that was open at 1:30 a.m. where I could buy Lorrie some ice cream. Finding it, I then drove all the way to Colorado Springs to give it to her. By the time I knocked on her door to give her the ice cream, it was already 3:00 a.m.

Wasn't that romantic! But that's what passion will do. When we're that much in love, we don't need to sleep. Looking googly-eyed at each other is much more important, and we can always sleep later.

Then, we are told, our bodies actually build up a resistance to this internally-produced drug, just like they do to any drug use, and more and more of it is necessary to achieve the same high. Ultimately the drug goes away and is replaced by something called endorphins. Rather than the hard-driving high the former drug gave us, this one gives us a soft and warm feeling. And suddenly we, who have vowed never to lose the intensity of romantic feeling experienced in courtship, find ourselves much less passionate. It is then that loving discipline must take over and make things happen that once happened automatically.

Why is it that so few married couples now plan dates with each other?

I am convinced that dating must be a regular part of our continued life together. Some no longer date because they never really developed a close friendship and actually prefer to be with other people who are their friends. Developing a close friendship should be one of the goals of our dating period. If sex is all we have to hold us together, a very important element is missing in our relationship. Anytime a couple does not have a strong desire to spend time with each other, they are in trouble.

Surprisingly, many wives don't want to spend time with their husbands, and husbands don't want to spend time with their wives. They would rather be anywhere than with their spouse. Each one, therefore, develops a completely independent circle of friends. This is very dangerous to the future health of the marriage.

Men have the mistaken idea that if they spend time with their wife, they will look henpecked. Then look henpecked, and if your friends don't understand it, that's okay. Godly men, real men, do all that they can to promote romanticism within their marriage. Doing something with Lorrie that is romantic has nothing to do with my manhood. It has everything to do with my love for my wife.

Newly single people often have a problem finding a suitable mate because they have forgotten how to date, and that is an indictment on modern marriage. Marriage should consist of constant dating. Part of the needed romance is treating your spouse as if you were on a date with them all the time.

Why is it so difficult for married couples to be alone and to have to look into each other's eyes and hearts?

Remember that cartoon I spoke of in an earlier chapter? In the first frame, the couple, out to dinner together, was holding hands across the table and saying to each other, "Isn't it great that the kids are away for the weekend?" In the next frame, one of them was looking out one window, and the other was looking out another window. And in the final frame, they had turned back to look at each other, and said, "So, when will the kids be back?" The activities surrounding their daily life had forced them apart, and without the children present, they seemed to have nothing in common to talk about.

All of us must guard against busyness, what some are calling "hecticness." It's a killer.

When we think of the word *intimacy*, we might break it down in this way: into me see. When we are being romantic with each other, looking into each other's eyes, we get to see who that person really is. As we noted in an earlier chapter, it is said that the eyes are the windows to the soul. So, by looking intensely into the eyes, you are seeing a person's soul. This creates an intimacy like nothing else can.

Why should this be so difficult for those who have been married for many years? In some ways, they seem to have become strangers to each other. They don't even know who the other person is anymore.

In his book *The Drifting Marriage*, Donald Harvey[25] makes some interesting statements. Among them, he says that there are three stages to a marriage: times of crisis, times of calmness, and times of busyness (or, as he puts it, "hecticness").

Crises tend to draw us together—unless, of course, it's the death of a child, and that can cause a severe strain on the relationship. Times of calm are when we can build a relationship. The hectic or busy times drive us apart. "Hecticness," will chew us up, spit us out, and quickly destroy a relationship.

Not only does the hectic pace of life often prevent us from finding time to be alone together. When we are together, we are troubled to find that there are new tensions between us. This happened to Lorrie and me after we had flown together to a much-anticipated retreat in Cancun, Mexico.

It's very easy to get too busy to enjoy each other.

I had been very busy for so long that I was really looking forward to lying on the beach and allowing the old familiar warm feelings to flow over me. When it didn't happen, I became concerned.

I had taken along my copy of *The Drifting Marriage,* and as I lay there reading it, I began to realize how very much it spoke to me personally. "Hey," I said to Lorrie, "this is a really good book."

A little later I turned to her again and said, "I'm finding some pieces of me in this book."

About an hour later, I said to her, "This is me."

We were in a calm place where we should have been building our relationship, and yet I felt estranged from Lorrie because of the busyness of our daily lives. When I voiced this to her, it frightened her. But over the next several nights we spent lots of time together and reconnected.

It's very easy to get too busy to enjoy each other. After all, the children have piano lessons and soccer practice, and we have church activities, business activities, and social activities. By Sunday evening we all fall into bed exhausted, and we haven't had the quality time we wanted to spend with each other during the week.

We can know that we're in trouble when we no longer want to go out to eat alone, just the two of us, or when we no longer want to go on vacation by ourselves. We would rather take some friends with us. Some couples I counsel with say that it has been years since they did anything together alone. That's not good.

Why, in some marriages, does life seem so dull, even boring?

I have never understood it, but some couples tell me that their relationship is wracked with boredom. This must mean that their marriage has become routine. They do the same things every day trying to treat each other with common politeness, but the passion has gone out of it, and there is no investment of energy or creativeness.

Couples like these are just going through the motions. They wake up in the morning, only to face the same daily routine and then fall into bed at night, exhausted from it all. If we treated our jobs like we treat our marriage relationship, we would have been fired a long time ago.

When we have put out energy all day long for other things, sometimes there just isn't anything left for the marriage. It is the last demand on us, and all too often we come up short. So, we just take each other for granted.

It is up to each partner to set boundaries in this regard. If I take Lorrie for granted, it's because she lets me do it. She needs to stop me and say something. She can't afford to permit that to happen.

Getting Our Priorities Straight

Sometimes our priorities are out of line, and we need to reassess them. God has presented us with a priority scale in the Scriptures, and we must live by it. The list looks like this:

- Our Relationship with God

- Our Relationship with Our Spouse

- Our Relationship with Our Children

- Our Service to God

- Our Relationship with Extended Family and Friends

- Our Work

Our first priority is always our relationship with God. He said:

You shall have no other gods before me. Exodus 20:3

Love the Lord your God with all your heart and with all your soul and with all your strength. Deuteronomy 6:5

God and our relationship with Him must always come first. This is the time we spend with Him in the morning reading the Bible, time spent in quiet meditation with our Friend. This is very different from our service to God (which must be ranked separately).

Our second priority in relationships must be our spouse. Lorrie is second to me only after my relationship with God, and I am second to her only after her relationship with God. She, however, comes before the call of God on my life, which is part of my service to Him. She is more important than my being a pastor, for instance, or my singing in the choir. And your spouse comes before your responsibility to be an usher, a greeter, or a Sunday school teacher.

God and our relationship with Him must always come first.

A pastor called me from another city and asked if I would help him and his wife with their troubled marriage. "Pastor," I said, "before I commit to that, I need to ask you a question: Are you willing to give up your church for your wife?"

"No way, man!" he answered.

"Then call me when you *are* willing," I suggested.

I was not saying that God would require him to give up his church, only that he had to be willing to do it. I know that this is the correct thing to do because God has said:

For this reason a man will leave his father and mother and be united to his wife, and they will become one flesh. Genesis 2:24

When we became *"one flesh,"* we become inseparable. We're one. This means that it is not correct for me to place anything between the two of us.

If I were to decide to insert something else between part of my body and me, I would endanger my very existence. In the same way, nothing can come between me and my spouse because we are one. If God calls me, then I have to wait until He calls her too. And He will, because He never calls just half a person.

The ministry has been allowed to separate many couples, and when a wife pleads her case, the reply she inevitably receives is this: "You just don't understand the ministry." And with that, the husband brushes her aside and continues with his work.

A wife who is treated in this way understandably resents it and begins to shut down. Then her husband begins to resent her because she's always nagging at him. The result is that the marriage is destroyed, and then how can the two of them serve God?

The Scriptures give no indication that it is ever proper for either a husband or wife to leave a spouse to follow after God. They are to leave father and mother to follow God. They are to leave houses and lands to do the work of the Lord, and we are even to leave grown children (see Mark 10:29). But, never do the Scriptures instruct us to leave a spouse to follow God.[26]

Our third priority, after God and spouse, is our minor children. Neglect them to your own peril.

Fourth, comes my service to God. With these relationships taken care of properly, then I can dedicate myself to something else: for instance, being an usher, a greeter, or a pastor. If Lorrie were to say to me at any time, "The ministry has robbed us of the ability to build a life together, and it is bringing division between us," and I sensed that she really meant it, I would leave the ministry immediately in order to bring healing to our relationship.

I love my work as a pastor to pastors, and such a decision would be very difficult for me to make, but I know that it would be a right one. God, my wife, and my children come before any other activity—including the call of God.

After I have taken care of these relationships, then I can think about extended family and friends, and about all of the other people in my life.

Finally, at the bottom of my list comes work. This is interesting in that so many of us become workaholics and give our lives to our work. Even many Christians have gotten their priorities all wrong.

Our enemy, who always wants to kill, steal, and destroy (see John 10:10) seeks to turn our priorities upside down. He tells us that work comes first and then extended family and friends. Consequently, many of us spend long hours at work, spend time with friends and extended families, then spend any other time left serving at the church. When this is all accomplished, we are so burned out that we have nothing left to give, and our spouse and children have to make do with the leftovers.

Many people eventually don't even have time for a relationship with God, and when this has happened, the devil has won. We must not allow it to happen.

I was invited to speak at a singles' retreat once in Cannon Beach, Oregon, a lovely little coastal town. I visited with some of the singles who were attending the conference at 7:00 a.m. in the coffee shop, and afterward I talked around the breakfast table with others.

I spoke in a morning session, and again ministered around the lunch table with those who were seated with us.

In the afternoon, we went out together and walked a little around that wonderful resort community right on the beach, and as we walked, people stopped us on the street to ask questions.

That evening, we ate dinner with some different people, and there was, again, much discussion around the table. Later I spoke again, and many stood in line to talk with me afterward. By the time I got to our room late that night, I was emotionally and physically exhausted.

After we had gone to bed, Lorrie suddenly needed something that was on a dresser on my side of the bed but across the room, and she asked me if I would get it for her. My brain screamed out, "Can't you see that I'm emotionally and physically exhausted? Are your hands broken? Are your legs broken? Can't you get it yourself?"

I was able to get my brain and mouth to answer correctly, "Yes," and I got up and handed her whatever it was she needed. Then, I got back into bed again.

After a while, Lorrie needed something else from my side of the bed, and this time I just couldn't get my brain and mouth to come together properly. "Can't you get it yourself?" I asked.

Then guess what Lorrie said: "You have enough time and energy for everyone else, but you don't have enough energy for me."

My brain wanted to scream out, "Can't you see that I'm a pastor and that God called me to do this? And didn't He call you to be a supportive wife, to stand by me and walk by me and to help me in the ministry? Don't you understand?" But this time I got control of my mouth because I knew what my mouth wanted to say was wrong.

"You're absolutely right," I said, and I got up and handed her what she needed. I had been guilty of putting my service to God ahead of Lorrie, and that was inappropriate.

The next day held a very similar schedule for us, and I was busy all day long ministering to people. That evening, however, I made sure I kept back some freshness so that when I got back to the room, Lorrie would not have to eat leftovers.

Our relationship with God comes first, then our relationship with spouse and children, and then our service to God.

I was speaking in Michigan on this topic and a single mother told me that she had the following schedule: She dropped her children off at school each morning and then went to work herself. After work in the evening, she picked up her children from school, got them some fast food to eat in the car, and they went to the church to work until eleven o'clock that night. They would go home and fall into bed and get up the next day and do it all over again. "Are you telling me that my life is wrong?" she asked.

"Absolutely," I assured her. She wasn't married, so she wasn't neglecting a spouse, but she had elevated her service to God to the level of her relationship with God, and that relationship was suffering, as well as her relationship with her small children. Let's get our priorities straight.

Not having your priorities in order is like painting your car so that it looks great, but the engine doesn't run. Establishing and maintaining priorities is important. Don't overlook them.

Why do we spend so little time adoring, admiring, and appreciating each other?

The reason clearly is that we no longer adore, admire, and appreciate each other. We all did this for a long time when we were first in love, so why don't we do it now? If we could continue doing that, love would never die.

What does it mean to adore someone? I have grown to depend on the adoring look I get from Lorrie when she is in the audience anywhere I'm speaking. That look means everything to me. It feeds my spirit, and I draw from it.

You have to understand that Lorrie has heard me teach the same things over and over again, and she would have every reason to look bored with what I'm saying at times. But she never does. She never once has that I've-heard-it-all-before look on her face. Instead, her look says to me, "This is awesome!"

When I see that look, it is difficult to explain what it does inside of me. I know that she loves me because I see it in her eyes, and that strengthens me and encourages me to go forward.

Speaking through an interpreter at a pastors' conference in Mexico, I said something I had never said before: "I can tell the kind of husband you are by looking into your wife's eyes." No sooner had I said it than I saw a look of terror in the eyes of some of the pastors present. Afterward, a little lady approached me. "Pastor," she said in her limited English, "you good man."

"I can tell the kind of husband you are by looking into your wife's eyes."

"Oh," I responded. "How do you know that?'

"I look in your wife's eyes," she said, and I knew what she meant.

Anytime I don't see that look of adoration in Lorrie's eyes, I get worried, and as soon as is practical or possible, I ask, "What's wrong?" I want to get that look back into her eyes as quickly as possible. I need it.

How can we show one another adoration, admiration, and appreciation? Ask your partner. They know what they need to hear or see.

Then consider this: If I were a mouse in the corner of the room, or if I followed you around, would I know that you adore your spouse? What would I see or hear that would indicate it? Could I tell by your actions? Could I tell by your words? Could I see it in your eyes? Or would I read disgust and boredom there?

How would you like to hear words like these?

How delightful is your love…my bride! How much more pleasing is your love than wine, and the fragrance of your perfume than any spice! Your lips drop sweetness as the honeycomb, my bride; milk and honey are under your tongue. The fragrance of your garments is like that of Lebanon. Song of Solomon 4:10-11

That's how God wants us to speak to each other.

What has happened to romance? When did we decide that we no longer needed to treat each other with the care and specialness we once demonstrated?

We need to take note of how the Bible expresses this important area of our lives.

Most people would not allow their children to read the Song of Solomon (also called the Song of Songs), because it is so sexually explicit, and yet this is the example God Himself has left for us in His Holy Word.

Our experience with romance and sexuality was so important to God that He devoted one of the sixty-six books in the Bible to this topic. He wrote a book that would be relevant to all generations to the end of time, and in it, He thought it was important enough to give explicit and frank instructions so that we could not miss His message.

This message from God shows us that we need to be passionate about our love for one another and that we need to express that passion. Why is it that we can compliment almost anyone around us, and yet we fail to compliment our spouse? How is it that we can show appreciation for most anyone and everyone around us, and yet we continually take our spouse for granted? Do you even look at your spouse anymore? Do you even notice them?

If your spouse turned up missing one day, would you be able tell the police what they were wearing or describe what they looked like? Have you noticed lately?

We once held a sweetheart banquet, and we separated the men and the women and then asked them questions about each other. Many of them had been married for ten or fifteen years or longer. We asked one man who had been married for fourteen years what color his wife's eyes were, and he didn't know.

One man confessed to me, "For many years now, I've taken my wife's elegance for granted. Today I realize what a treasure she is, and I will never neglect her in this way again."

If you have what you need at home, then you'd better learn to appreciate it, or it may suddenly vanish into thin air and be gone one day. We have all seen men with gorgeous wives looking around at other women, and we wondered, "What's wrong with him?" We have known women who had good husbands, and yet they were unsatisfied, and we wondered, "Why doesn't she appreciate what she has?" We need to take inventory and make sure we're not in danger of making the same mistake.

The Basic Differences Between How Men and Women View Romance

There are some basic differences between men and women and the way they approach the whole issue of romance. Men see romance and sex as a continuum, and they expect to move seamlessly from one to the other. Women, on the other hand, don't see that natural progression. At the end of a special evening, a woman will make a decision as to whether the evening will naturally progress to lovemaking with her husband. Men don't understand anything about that decision. To us, it's the natural thing to do.

Men, we need to understand and respect our wife's desires romantically, and women, you need to understand and honor your husband's perspective on romance.

Men, your wife needs to hear words of love and caring from you. She needs to be romanced. Women, you need to learn that if you throw in a little sex on the side with your romance, you have your man hooked.

Poetically speaking, romance is the flame which glows on the candle of unconditional love. Try memorizing that, guys, and at just the right moment, spring it on your wife. That will earn you some brownie points for sure.

Romance is the fertile soil in which passion grows, and when you are romantic with your wife, it prevents her from believing that sex is all you ever think about. Most women are of the opinion that all we men want is to get them into the bedroom, and that's our fault. We haven't learned to show them love and devotion as we should. Romance is what we should be doing every waking hour of every waking day—whether it has sex connected with it or not.

Romance, then, is the act of keeping your courtship alive long after the wedding day, and there are no substitutes for it.

The problem is that what is romantic to men is not always romantic to women. Take, for instance, the man who went to romance class and read *1001 Ways to Be Romantic* and then started looking for ways to put what he had learned into action. Behind their house was a mountain, and he decided that it would be simply awesome if he were somehow able to arrange a romantic dinner for the two of them on the very top of that mountain.

One morning before work he carried a table and two chairs to the top of the mountain. Then he trudged back up with all of the necessary food and stored it nearby. He placed a white tablecloth on the table and candles to be lighted at the right moment. The table was gorgeous in that setting, and he was sure that she would love it.

He even arranged for a violin player to go up the mountain at just the right time and to begin playing softly from a distance. He had put a lot of effort into planning his romantic dinner, and he was very excited about it all day long.

The only problem was that when his wife came home from work that evening, she had been on her feet all day, and they were hurting. When she heard her husband's proposal, "Let's take a little romantic stroll up the mountain," it sounded like the worst idea she had ever heard in her life.

Seeing how important it was to him, she decided that she simply had to pull herself together and muster up the strength to please him. After a while, she got herself ready, and they started up the mountain.

They had to stop often so that she could rest, and he had to half drag her up the final slopes of the mountain. Still, he was excited. And this excitement grew as they finally neared the spot where he had set everything up hours before. He could hardly contain himself. This was going to be GREAT!

Of course, it didn't turn out that way. The violin player had been there for some time already, and although he had not left, he was clearly not very happy about their late arrival. The beautiful table setting was in a shambles. The wind had knocked it over, and everything was scattered here and there.

Worst of all, to the man, his wife was not feeling at all romantic. She had had no idea why he was insisting that she take this hike in the mountains after her hard day's work. And she certainly had not been anticipating anything like this. What he had visualized as being so romantic turned out to be a total disaster.

This is not uncommon. Since the old saying, opposites attract, is true, romantic people often marry non-romantic people, just as stingy people marry spendthrifts and strict disciplinarians marry people who are more lenient with their children. That's just how it is.

Women are more prone to be romantics than men, but sometimes the role is reversed. I am the romantic in our household, and I have had my share of disasters in this regard.

One day I was leafing through a catalog, and I spotted an awesome ad for a shower head. It read: "Starlighted Shower Head: Generates Light Using Water Power." The price was fifty dollars, and although I didn't have fifty dollars to spend on a shower head, I thought the idea was so awesome that we just had to have one. So, unbeknownst to Lorrie, I ordered one and paid for it out of my allowance.

The Starlighted Shower Head finally arrived, and one day, while Lorrie was still at work, I set about to install it and have it operational when she got home. We have always showered together, and I was planning to suggest an early shower for us.

It was the time of year when it got dark early, so I turned out the lights and had the special shower head ready when Lorrie came in. It would give off a glow that cascaded down on everything around it, and I thought that would be VERY romantic.

When the moment came, I stepped first into the shower and turned the water on. The shower head began to make a soft whirring sound as the built-in generator, as advertised, began to cast a soft red glow over everything. I was so excited. I just knew Lorrie was going to love it.

As she stepped into the shower, she said "Why is it so dark in here? Turn the lights on. And, what is that noise?" And, just that quickly my balloon burst.

It would have been very easy for me the next time I felt like doing something romantic to draw back and be cautious. "Don't do it," I could have told myself. "You'll only make a fool of yourself. It isn't worth the risk." After all, I had spent fifty hard-saved allowance dollars on the shower of my dreams, and Lorrie hadn't appreciated it at all. Should I now risk more?

But the risk was more than money. Could I risk becoming vulnerable again and open that area that could so easily be hurt by rejection? It might be hard, but I must do it.

Of course, Lorrie had not purposely rained on my parade, but those who are the non-romantics of the family need to become sensitive to the feelings of the one who goes out of their way to prepare a romantic evening or weekend. It is very easy to say: "Why did you go to all of this bother? We could have eaten at home and avoided all of this hassle. What's wrong with our own dining room? If you wanted candles, you could have lit them there."

To the practical partner, this would seem to be the logical thing to say. "It needs to be said," we might even be thinking. But if our words cause the romantic partner to draw back the next time and make them reluctant to climb life's mountains to show them love, that would be a tragedy.

What would have been a proper response from the surprised and dismayed wife of the young man who prepared dinner at the top of the mountain? "Oh, what an awesome view, and what a lot of effort you put into all of this. Thank you for setting it up just for me. I'm so sorry it didn't work out as you planned, but it was incredible of you to think of it." That would have softened the blow.

What Is Romantic and What Isn't?

I used to tease Lorrie, telling her that her idea of a really romantic outfit was to put on her flannel pajamas. Of course, that was not romantic to me at all. I love to buy her fancy lingerie from Victoria's Secret® to wear. She tells me that I'm not shopping for her, but for me. And, of course, she's right.

Over time, Lorrie has learned to appreciate my desire for her and tries to remember to wear her fancy things on occasion—just for me. When she doesn't remember (and that's easy because it's not important to her), I feel the hurt that many romantics experience. Often enough she realizes that I buy these things out of my love for her, and she accepts my gifts with grace.

Men, because of our tendency to equate romance with sex, it's a good idea to have your wife make a list of what she considers to be romantic. Some of the things Lorrie wrote on her list, for instance, were the following:

- You singing a love song to me in our room at night. (This didn't happen often because I don't have a public singing voice.)

- You asking me how I am and really wanting to know.

- Seeing you listening to the feelings of the children with gentleness. (This didn't seem very romantic to me, but it was to her.)

- You writing a warm letter to my folks.

- Me coming to bed and finding you sitting there with your pajama bottoms wrapped in a turban around your head and a silly grin on your face.

- You putting my interests first.

- Seeing you humble yourself around others.

194

Many of these don't seem romantic to us men at all, but with our wives, romance is a totally different concept. Keep those lists handy, men, and refer to them often. It will help you.

If a man would make a list of what's romantic, it would be something like this:

- Making love on a deserted beach.

- Making love under water.

- Making love in the woods.

- Making love covered with whipped cream.

- Making love in an elevator.

Her list might also have this type of thing:

- Seeing him getting the children excited about a Bible story.

- The whole family together throwing rocks in a stream.

- Walking together through the leaves on an autumn afternoon.

- Praying together.

Now, that's romantic to a woman.

So, guys, if you go shopping at Victoria's Secret,® and you buy something, you're not really buying it for her; you're buying it for you. Ask her to wear it, but know that it's for your benefit. Then give her the kind of romantic things she needs from you.

You cannot afford to give her what seems romantic to you. That won't work. What you define as romantic is not always romantic to her, so don't be angry or hurt when she doesn't respond as you expect her to.

To a man, making love on a beach is something to look forward to. To the wife, all she can think about is how uncomfortable the sand would be. "You want to do what?" she asks.

To him, a sexy negligee is romantic. To her, it might seem ridiculous. This presents an opportunity for serious hurt.

One very attractive woman on her wedding night put on a beautiful, white, very romantic negligee and came proudly into the marital bedroom. When her bridegroom saw her, he laughed and said, "That reminds me of my mother's curtains." Years later, when they came to me for counseling, she was still trying to get over the hurt of that first "romantic" experience with her new husband.

Throwing cold water on each other's feelings of romanticism is not wise.

Throwing cold water on each other's feelings of romanticism is not wise. It would not have hurt that man to say and to mean, "You look absolutely radiant tonight."

Some people's idea of romanticism is to leave a trail of clothes from the front door to the bedroom. That might seem perfectly disgusting to their mate, but to the romantic, it builds anticipation.

I came home one night to find all the lights out and a trail of roses that I was obviously meant to follow. The trail led into the bedroom, around the corner and into the bathroom. There I found a hot bubble bath Lorrie had prepared for me. That was a wonderful, romantic end to a stressful day.

If you find clothes strewn from the front door to the bedroom and there you find her fully dressed, that would be a cruel hoax. For my part, I would not like to find Lorrie in her flannel nightgown at the end of such a trail of clothing.

For some women, a really romantic evening would be to sit together and look at wedding pictures and, thus, relive the nostalgia of that blissful day. The husband might say something like, "Haven't we seen these before? Do we need to do this again?" Oh, shut up. If it's romantic to her, then you need to participate in a loving, caring way.

Some find it romantic to scatter rose petals over the bed. The non-romantic will tend to say, "What a mess! Where's the vacuum cleaner? It will take us forever to get this mess cleaned up." Resist the temptation. If it's important to your spouse, invest honest, emotional energy into learning to appreciate their language of romance.

It thrills me to find love notes lying about, although some might not find that to be very romantic at all.

Many say to me, "But I'm not very creative." That may be true, but there are many helpful resources available to give you more ideas on how to be romantic, and we should use all of the resources available to us. Do whatever you have to do to keep your passion fresh and flowing. Don't take the chance that love will die and then have to be revived.

Look for resources on the Internet. Buy a good book on the subject. Don't be afraid to encourage a mate who is stepping out in search of new ideas because, to many, stepping into the romantic can be a rather scary experience.

Do it because you love your mate. Do it because you want your marriage to last. Do it because you appreciate what God has given you and you don't want to risk losing it. And if and when your mate is taking these steps, be careful not to offend them and send them backward.

Lorrie has always considered herself to be creative in many ways, except in romance and sexuality, and yet early on in our relationship she determined to learn ways to keep our love fresh and alive. Because she had a girlfriend who was very talented in this area, she decided to take lessons from her. This friend became her coach, and Lorrie learned many wonderful ideas from her.

At first, the ideas seemed a bit too radical for Lorrie's tastes, but when she tried them on me and I liked them, she decided to make learning new things a lifelong experience. Pleasing me pleases her, and it means a lot to me just to know that she thinks enough of me to make the effort to work so hard at it.

We were in Canada for a few days of vacation together and were on an island in the middle of a lake alone. I was surprised when a Little Red Riding Hood who wasn't wearing much suddenly jumped out from behind a tree and handed me a big-bad-wolf mask. That was romantic!

One time I was teaching a five-part series on sexuality to our Sunday school class, and I asked Lorrie to teach one of the sessions from a female perspective. During that class, she suggested to the ladies that they meet their husbands at the door some evening with nothing on but Saran Wrap.® On the way home, I told her I thought it had been a great idea. Several months later on a trip to Florida for my birthday, she trumped up some excuse for me to go to the hotel lobby. When I returned, she met me in our room with, you guessed it, nothing on but wonderful, clear Saran Wrap.®

What a sight! To me, that was very romantic!

Put some spice back into your relationship. Let your mate know that they are loved and appreciated and that you still find them attractive.

If you can afford it, hire a masseuse to come to your home and give your spouse a professional massage. One night I had a lady come quietly to the back door with her equipment. She set up the table, and when Lorrie came in, the masseuse was ready to give her a massage.

Lorrie wasn't worth much after that. She was a limp rag, and fell into bed and went to sleep. But she deserved that, and it let her know how much I loved her.

Guys, go out and start your wife's car on cold winter mornings. That may not feel very romantic to you, but it can feel very romantic to her when she doesn't have to get into a cold car.

Romance doesn't begin late at night on the way to the bedroom. It begins when you get out of bed in the morning. If it only happens in the evening, it feels false to her. It seems manipulative. The little things that you can do for her all day long make all the difference in the world. That lets her know that you don't have a one-track mind.

When was the last time you wrote a love letter to your wife? Oh, I know it's not easy, but it's worth it.

Lorrie told me one day that she would find it very romantic if I would write her a love letter, so I got a pen and paper and sat down to get started. I sat there for a while, trying to pull my thoughts together and chewing on the pen. Then I chewed the pen some more, and I chewed the pen some more.

Nothing that I thought of sounded right to me. It wasn't good enough. When Lorrie had suggested that I write a love letter, it had sounded so easy, but when I actually tried to do it, I found that it was not easy at all. I was not very good at waxing poetic, and nothing that came to me seemed to express deeply enough what I felt about her.

Eventually I did pull the letter together, but it took me a long time, and I wasn't happy with the outcome. Years later, I found that letter on my computer, and we read it over together. Amazingly, it sounded pretty good to us both. "Wow! I didn't do so bad after all." I exulted. It had taken me a long time to write because it is never easy for me to wax poetic.

Call your wife at work and ask, "Is this the office of the most beautiful woman in the world?"

"Can I help you?" she'll say.

And you can answer, "Oh, can you!!!"

Put a love note in your husband's pocket, and when he puts his hand in there to get something, he'll be pleasantly surprised.

Your note could say something as simple as, "I just wanted you to know how much I love you." There's not a man anywhere in the world, no matter how macho, who would not be moved by that.

When you can afford it, you can buy her a diamond necklace, but don't feel badly if you cannot afford it. She knows what you can and can't afford. Reminisce with her about the past. Take a walk together down memory lane. Just enjoy each other's presence. Shower together by candlelight. Warm her bath towel in the dryer.

Lorrie was born with cold feet. They're even cold in the summertime. I have learned to keep a hair dryer under the edge of our bed so that I can warm her feet with it. Sometimes I warm up the whole bed just before she gets into it, and that makes her very content. It's a small thing, and it doesn't cost me anything. So why not do it?

Truth be told, I have an ulterior motive. The older I get the harder it is for me to have Lorrie put her cold feet on me. Warming her feet has no sexual connotation, but it is very romantic to her. In fact, as I reported earlier, this was the thing she remembered as the most romantic thing I had done for her in months at one point.

Cuddle together in front of a campfire or a fireplace because women love cuddling. And, men, don't be too hasty to take it to another level. Be willing to do what she enjoys.

Pulling It All Together

Romance doesn't just happen naturally in a marriage. Passion runs out when the PCP-like drug stops being produced. And then you have to sit down and think what you should do. Doing moon eyes at each other will no longer happen naturally. You have to make it happen. The other romantic things you did out of instinct now will have to be done with thoughtful purpose. Make them happen.

Romance is not simply an extension of physical intimacy. The winning recipe for romance is found in developing a friendship centered on shared interests and is carefully planned. As you walk together, he can ask her about her potted plants, and she can ask him about the outcome of the weekend's football games. Stop to share interests.

While Lorrie and I were in Mexico a couple of years ago, we were reading an interesting book by John Gotman entitled *Seven Reasons Why Relationships Work*.[27] One of the chapters, called "Life Mapping," was so intriguing that we sat with it over dinner one evening. At the end of each chapter were questions, and the questions at the end of that particular chapter were designed to help you discover more about your spouse. It was amazing how much we learned about each other in a very short time. For instance, I had never known that Lorrie's favorite color was royal blue or that her favorite flower was the lily.

The book suggested that you talk with your mate about the three things that most cause you stress and that you then listen to your mate describe the three things that most cause them stress. In this way, you can get to know each other better, and the exchange of ideas about life can be very romantic.

Often, Lorrie and I ask each other what the three highs and three lows were for our day, or we talk about a trip or some other interesting experience. We try to share the things we have most enjoyed and also the more unpleasant parts of any experience. This keeps us in touch with each other.

Use the element of surprise to keep your romantic life fresh. Be spontaneous and creative.

When your mate attempts to surprise you, don't disappoint them. Act surprised. Go along for the ride, and you just might enjoy it.

Spontaneity is okay. Not everything has to be planned in advance. If it is something as important as an anniversary celebration, you might want to plan that together. Or you can ask your partner's permission for you to plan it and surprise them with the details.

Part of being romantic is taking time to plan special things, putting some thought and effort into it.

Don't always do the same things in the same way. If, when I came home every night, I found roses leading to the bathroom, I might quickly get tired of that. Do something else. If you're not creative yourself, seek help.

Lorrie and I take turns each year planning something special for our anniversary. She does it one year, and I do it the next. We do the same thing with our date night. She plans them for one week or one month, and I plan them for the next. We also make use of wonderful resources. One of our favorites is *Simply Romantic Nights* by Dennis and Barbara Rainy.[28] It has plans for twenty-four nights, twelve for the husband and twelve for the wife, and it gives you detailed instructions, from how to plan the proper setting to what to do about arranging for someone to care for any minor children.

The book has an inventory sheet that each of you fills out. This contains such questions as: What is your favorite candy? What is your favorite flower? You can fill it out and exchange it with your spouse, and then they will know more about how to plan. It's a great resource.

Finally, make sure you give your full, undivided attention to your loved one during a romantic interval. It is not a time to talk about the plumbing problem or to be watching television out of the corner of your eye. If you're having a romantic dinner together at a restaurant, it's not the time to be noticing who walks by.

When your mate attempts to surprise you, don't disappoint them. Act surprised.

You're looking for connectedness, and nothing must be allowed to spoil that connectedness. Look at your mate. Notice how attractive they are, and concentrate on them.

Every night, without exception, as I'm lying in bed beside Lorrie, I thank God for her and the precious gift she is to me. I thank Him that He has provided this wonderful relationship for the both of us.

And that is where our romanticism begins—with our walk with God. It is God who created within us the capacity for romanticism. It is His love that makes us free to enjoy each other, to be unrestricted and not feel any shame, to give ourselves to each other in open abandonment.

In gratitude to Him and in obedience to His commands, I give myself fully to Lorrie. I concern myself with learning what seems romantic to her, and then I make the effort to do it. Once she tells me what she finds romantic, then I have no excuse.

Ladies, your job is even easier. Learn to add an extra edge of sexuality to your romanticism, and your husband will love you for it.

By focusing on God first, we take the focus off of ourselves and what is important to us, and then His love in us causes us to want to please our spouse. And this is a formula for success in the marriage. Do it now *Before Love Dies.*

Endnotes

1. Vinton, Bobby (New York, NY) Epic, 1968.

2. Harvey, Donald. *The Drifting Marriage.* Ada, Michigan: Fleming H. Revell, 1988.

3. Peck, Scott. *The Road Less Traveled.* New York: Simon & Schuster, 2002.

4. Harley, Willard. *His Needs Her Needs,* Grand Rapids: Baker Books, 2001.

5. Smalley, Gary and Norma. *If Only He Knew.* Grand Rapids: Zondervan, 1997.

6. Chapman, Gary. *The Five Love Languages.* Chicago: Northfield Publishing, 1992.

7. Smalley, Gary with Trent, John. *Love Is a Decision.* Dallas, Texas: Word Publishing, 1989.

8. Dillow, Linda and Pintus, Lorraine. *Intimate Issues.* Colorado Springs: Waterbrook Press, 1999.

9. Weir, Terry and Carruth, Mark. *Holy Sex.* New Kensington, Pennsylvania: Whitaker House Publishers, 1999.

10. Weir, Terry and Carruth, Mark. *Holy Sex.* New Kensington, Pennsylvania: Whitaker House Publishers, 1999.

11. Wilson, Bunny. *Liberated Through Submission: God's Design for Freedom in All Relationships.* Eugene, Oregon: Harvest House Publishers, 1998.

12. Leman, Kevin. *Sex Begins in the Kitchen.* Ada, Michigan: Fleming H. Revell, 1999.

13. Wheat, Ed. *Intended for Pleasure*. Ada, Michigan: Fleming H. Revell, 1981, Revised 1997.

14. Dillow, Linda and Pintus, Lorraine. *Intimate Issues*. Colorado Springs: Waterbrook Press, 1999.

15. Penner, Clifford and Joyce. *The Gift of Sex*. Nashville: W. Publishing Group, 2003.

16. Weir, Terry and Carruth, Mark. *Holy Sex*. New Kensington, Pennsylvania: Whitaker House Publishers, 1999.

17. Out of print.

18. Cloud, Henry and Townsend, John. *Safe People*. Grand Rapids: Zondervan, 1996.

19. Powell, John. *Why Am I Afraid to Tell You Who I Am?* Allen, Texas: Thomas More Publishing, 1996.

20. Author unknown.

21. Gleaned from a handout given to us in a graduate class on Sociology at the University of Colorado.

22. Wilson, Bunny. *Liberated Through Submission: God's Design for Freedom in All Relationships*. Eugene, Oregon: Harvest House Publishers, 1998.

23. Wilson, Bunny. *Liberated Through Submission: God's Design for Freedom in All Relationships*. Eugene, Oregon: Harvest House Publishers, 1998.

24. Peck, Scott. *The Road Less Traveled*. New York: Simon & Schuster, 2002.

25. Harvey, Donald. *The Drifting Marriage*. Ada, Michigan: Fleming H. Revell, 1988.

26. Although the KJV of the Bible and the NKJV use the word *"wife,"* the Interlinear Greek Bible offers this explanation: "This word was added by the translators for better readability in the English. There is no actual word in the Hebrew/Greek text. (Biblesoft's New Exhaustive Strong's Numbers and Comcordance with Expanded Greek-Hebrew Dictionary, copyright © 1994, Biblesoft and Internationa Bible Translators, Inc.)

27. Gottman, John. *Seven Principles for Making Relationships Work*. New York, NY: Three Rivers Press, 2000.

28. Rainy, Dennis and Barbara. *Simply Romantic Nights*. Little Rock, Arkansas, FamilyLife, 1990.

Bibliography

Chapman, Gary. *The Five Love Languages.* Chicago: Northfield Publishing, 1992.

Cloud, Henry and Townsend, John. *Safe People.* Grand Rapids: Zondervan, 1996.

Cunningham, Will. *How to Enjoy a Family Fight.* Phoenix, Arizona: Questar Publishers, 1988.

Dillow, Linda and Pintus, Lorraine. *Intimate Issues.* Colorado Springs: Waterbrook Press, 1999.

Godek, Gregory J. P. *1001 Ways to Be Romantic.* Weymouth, Massachusetts: Casablanca Press, 1995.

Gottman, John. *Seven Principles for Making Relationships Work.* New York, NY: Three Rivers Press, 2000.

Harley, Willard. *His Needs, Her Needs.* Grand Rapids: Baker Books, 2001.

Hart, Archibald and Catherine and Taylor, Debra L. *Secrets of Eve: Understanding the Mystery of Female Sexuality.* Nashville, Tennessee: Word Publishing, 1998.

Harvey, Donald. *The Drifting Marriage.* Ada, Michigan: Fleming H. Revell, 1988.

Leman, Kevin. *Sex Begins in the Kitchen*. Ada, Michigan: Fleming H. Revell, 1999.

Peck, Scott. *The Road Less Traveled*. New York: Simon and Schuster, 2002.

Penner, Clifford and Joyce. *Getting Your Sex Life Off to a Great Start*. Dallas, Texas: Word Publishing, 1994.

Penner, Clifford and Joyce. *The Gift of Sex*. Nashville: W. Publishing Group, 2003.

Powell, John. *Why Am I Afraid to Tell You Who I Am?*. Allen, Texas: Thomas More Publishing, 1996.

Rainey, Dennis and Barbara. *Building Your Mate's Self-Esteem*. San Bernardino, California: Here's Life Publishers, 1986.

Rainy, Dennis and Barbara. *Simply Romantic Nights*. Little Rock, Arkansas: FamilyLife, 1990.

Smalley, Gary. *If Only He Knew*. Grand Rapids: Zondervan, 1997.

Smalley, Gary with Trent, John. *Love Is a Decision*. Dallas, Texas: Word Publishing, 1989.

Wheat, Ed. *Intended for Pleasure*. Ada, Michigan: Fleming H. Revell, 1981, Revised 1997.

Wier, Terry with Carruth, Mark. *Holy Sex: God's Purpose and Plan for Our Sexuality*. New Kensington, PA: Whitaker House, 1999.

Wilson, Bunny. *Liberated Through Submission: God's Design for Freedom in All Relationships*. Eugene, Oregon: Harvest House Publishers, 1998.

www.legacypublishersinternational.com